A Reference Guide to

CLEAN AIR

CASS R. SANDAK

◆Science, Technology, and Society Reference Series ◆

ENSLOW PUBLISHERS, INC.

Bloy St. & Ramsey Ave.	P.O. Box 38
Box 777	Aldershot
Hillside, N.J. 07205	Hants GU12 6BP
U.S.A.	U.K.

Library of Congress Cataloging-in-Publication Data

Sandak, Cass R.
    A Reference Guide to Clean Air.
    (Science, technology, and society reference series)
    Summary: Discusses the many environmental problems, in alphabetical
order, that are presently plaguing our air and atmosphere.
    1. Air—Pollution—Dictionaries, Juvenile. 2. Air quality
management—Dictionaries, Juvenile. [1. Air—Pollution—Dictionaries] I.
Title. II. Series.

TD883.13.S26   1990   363.73'92'003   89-25601

ISBN 0-89490-261-X

Printed in the United States of America

10 9 8 7 6 5 4 3 2 1

For my father

CONTENTS

INTRODUCTION

It is hardly possible to pick up a newspaper, open a magazine, or turn on the radio or television without finding the word POLLUTION. Acid rain, smog, global warming, ozone layer depletion, and the greenhouse effect are all buzzwords relating to the worldwide problem of air pollution. The condition of our planet is of such importance that *Time* magazine named the Endangered Earth as its annual "Person of the Year" for 1988.

The air that surrounds our planet is becoming increasingly polluted by contaminants that threaten our health and well-being. Contaminants in food, water, and soil are just part of the overall problem. But the contaminated atmosphere is everyone's concern.

The air we breathe is filled with hazardous substances. Sometimes we are aware of them because we can smell an unusual odor. Other pollutants are not so easy to detect. Scientists have devised systems to find out what is in the air we breathe. They continually monitor the condition of the atmosphere by taking air samples and making careful tests and measurements.

Many air pollutants have strange and unfamiliar names. But even chemicals whose names are obscure may be present in smoke from fires at the local dump or in emissions from industrial smokestacks. Accidents at chemical factories or power plants may release large quantities of harmful substances that may ordinarily be present in the air in only small amounts.

Air pollution became a real problem only after the start of the industrial era. Every manufacturing process is linked to some form of air pollution, and industry today sends millions of tons of pollutants into the atmosphere each year. Since its first appearance at the beginning of the twentieth century, the automobile also has been a major source of pollution.

Even natural processes have important atmospheric consequences. Natural sources of pollution include the actions of volcanoes, lightning, the movement of the ocean, the weathering of rocks and minerals, respiration, photosynthesis, pollination, the decomposition of organic matter, digestion, evaporation, and plant chemistry.

Sometimes substances that contaminate the atmosphere are components of ordinary air. But when the proportions of these parts of the atmosphere change, they too may become threatening. The build-up of carbon dioxide, methane, and other heat-absorbing gases and the depletion of the ozone layer are examples of damage to the environment caused by natural substances. Human activity has disturbed their normal balance in the atmosphere.

The materials and processes that pollute the atmosphere affect many different things. Air pollution gases and particles damage trees and soil or ruin clothing and corrode buildings and other structures. They may also cause your eyes to water and hurt, your head to ache, or your nose to itch. Evidence links air pollution to respiratory and heart disease, allergies, and several types of cancer.

We know what many of the problems of the environment are. We also know something about what future troubles may occur. But what can we do about them?

This book is designed to show how the key issue of atmospheric contamination is affected by the interactions of science, technology, and society. This way of looking at the issue will give you a broad base of understanding to help you consider the problem of air pollution and decide what you can do about it.

Human efforts can make a big difference. In the years since the introduction of unleaded gasoline in 1975, there has been a 94 percent drop in the level of lead emissions that end up in the atmosphere. That is an area where a problem has been addressed and solved. Scrubbers and electrostatic precipitators are used on many industrial smokestacks. These devices help to keep pollutants out of the atmosphere. But almost all air pollution remedies are expensive, and the money has to come from somewhere.

The control of contaminating emissions is a desirable goal. But it adds to the cost of doing business. Industries are reluctant to set up pollution control systems unless it is clear that business operations are damaging human health. Therefore, governments in the United States and in many European countries have found it necessary to enact laws that hold industries legally accountable for the pollution damage they cause.

There is no question that human activities are changing the composition of the air we breathe. What the consequences of mankind's actions will be, however, is still unknown. This book may give you some of the information needed to help find the answers.

USING THE BOOK

The main portion of this book is an alphabetical listing of nearly 200 names, terms, and concepts that all have some relation to atmospheric contamination. This section is called **Air Terms.**

Chemicals are listed, giving their standard chemical symbols and formulas, properties, and characteristics. The entry then tells how these substances are pollutants and how they enter the atmosphere. Finally, the known health effects are briefly discussed.

Many of the entries contain cross-references. When certain concepts are dealt with in varying degrees in other articles, these references tell you where more information may be found.

The other sections of the book are designed as tools to aid in understanding the Air Terms section and to help you find more information on various topics:

Terms Used in the Field. This glossary includes explanations of common terms encountered in the study of air pollution. Most of them are used many times in the balance of the book.

Laws and Agencies. This part of the book includes a summary of much of the legislation that regulates pollutants and a partial listing of the many government departments that deal with the environment, particularly the atmosphere.

For Further Information. This section provides addresses of government and consumer agencies that will provide additional literature and information on specific air pollution topics.

References. This section includes a listing of many of the books used in the preparation of this work. It also includes a general listing of suggested newspapers and periodicals that publish solid current information about various phases of atmospheric pollution.

Sometimes entries in the Air Terms section contain numbers in parentheses. These numbers are keyed to the reference numbers in this section. The reference numbers show where to find additional information on certain important topics.

TERMS USED IN THE FIELD

ABSORPTION. The process of taking up and incorporating another substance. For example, liquids may absorb gases or particles.

ACID. An acid is a water-soluble compound that gives hydrogen ions to water to form hydronium ions. They react violently with some substances, releasing hydrogen gas. Acids have some properties that are opposite to those of bases. Vinegar is a weak acid. Sulfuric acid and hydrochloric acid are strong acids that can cause severe chemical burns.

ACIDITY. A measure of how much acid there is in a substance. Acidity is measured on a pH scale, which ranges from 0 to 14. (pH represents the degree of hydrogen ion activity.) Numbers from 0 to 7 represent acids; numbers from 7 to 14 represent bases. The number 7 itself is neutral—neither acid nor base. The lower the pH value, the higher the acidity.

ACUTE. Exposure to a substance that is short-term and intense. Or, a health effect that is severe but of short duration. Contrast with a long-term, or **CHRONIC**, effect or exposure.

ADSORPTION. One way that gaseous pollutants are removed from the air. Molecules of the contaminating substance chemically cling to the surface of a solid filtering material, such as activated charcoal.

AGENT. A substance able to produce a chemical or biological effect. Bacteria are disease-carrying agents.

ALKALINITY. The measure of strength of a base.

AMBIENT AIR. The air outdoors (in contrast to indoor air); the atmosphere in any particular location.

ASPHYXIATION. Death from lack of sufficient oxygen in the air, also known as suffocation. Air that is filled with carbon monoxide (or certain other gases) can asphyxiate since the blood cells' ability to carry oxygen is impaired.

BASE. A substance that will form hydroxide ions when dissolved in water. The word *alkaline* is often used to refer to a base.

BY–PRODUCT. A secondary substance, produced during a process. Sometimes the breakdown of a primary substance causes the by-product. In many cases, the by-product is an undesirable or unexpected result.

CARCINOGEN. Any substance that produces cancer. Labeling a substance as carcinogenic usually requires years of testing of animals exposed to the substance in controlled experiments. Animal findings are then compared with data obtained by observing human cancer cases.

CAUSTIC. Corrosive, usually applied to the power of bases (or alkalines) to damage human or animal tissues or other materials.

CENTRAL NERVOUS SYSTEM (CNS). The brain and spinal cord

in human beings and other animals that have backbones. It coordinates the activity of the other parts of the body.

CHEMICAL. A substance that may be an element, a compound, or a mixture. Many chemicals react with other substances to form new substances.

CHRONIC. Long-term exposure to a substance, or a long-term health effect. Contrast with a short-term, or **ACUTE,** effect or exposure.

COMBUSTION. The burning of wood or fossil fuels. During combustion, carbon and oxygen combine.

COMPOUND. A chemical substance containing atoms of two or more elements. The molecules of a compound contain fixed amounts of the chemical elements that form it. Water is one of the most common compounds. A molecule of water always has two atoms of hydrogen and one of oxygen.

CONTAMINANT. A substance in the air that is not naturally present or that is present in greater-than-normal quantities.

CORROSIVE. A chemical capable of wearing away or eating away another substance.

DEFOLIANT. A chemical substance that causes plants to lose their leaves.

EFFLUENT. A liquid or gas that flows out of something; for example, the waste gases from an industrial smokestack or the contaminated water released by a chemical process.

EMISSION RATE. An amount of pollutant released by a source in a specified length of time.

EVAPORATION. The changing of a liquid or solid into minute gas particles.

FUMIGANT. A substance whose chemical vapors are used to destroy pests such as rodents or insects. The substance may also be used to disinfect an area.

FUNGICIDE. A chemical that destroys fungi, including rusts, molds, rot, and mildew. These fungi may also cause injury to plants or other materials.

HERBICIDE. A chemical substance that kills vegetation. Defoliants are herbicides that cause the leaves of a plant to drop off but allow the roots to survive.

HYDROCARBONS. Compounds that contain only hydrogen and carbon.

INERT. Inactive or very slow to take part in chemical reactions.

INORGANIC. Chemical substances that do not contain carbon. Most inorganic substances come from inanimate sources.

LETHAL DOSE. A quantity of a substance capable of causing death.

MICROGRAM. The one millionth part of a gram. Since there are 454 grams in an English pound, a pound contains 454,000,000 milligrams.

MICRON. A unit of measure equal to one millionth part of a meter.

MICROORGANISMS (or **MICROBES**). Microscopic plants and animals that include tiny insects, viruses, fungi, and bacteria. Microorganisms in the air are one of the principal ways that diseases are spread.

MILLIGRAM. The one thousandth part of a gram.

MUTAGEN. A substance that changes the genetic material in an organism.

ORGANIC. Substances that come directly or indirectly from living things. Organic chemistry deals with compounds that contain carbon atoms.

OUTGASING. The production and seepage of gases from solid or liquid materials. Some plastics outgas toxic chemicals. Often building materials or insulation foams may outgas formaldehyde vapors.

PARTICULATE MATTER. A small particle that remains suspended in the air. Dust and ash in the air are examples of particulate matter.

PATHOGEN. A substance that causes disease. It is often a virus or bacterium. Sometimes a pathogen is a chemical agent, a respirable fiber, or other source of disease.

PHOTOSYNTHESIS. The chemical process by which green plants use water and carbon dioxide in the presence of sunlight to make simple sugars. Plants use the food made through photosynthesis for their own metabolism. The process releases oxygen into the atmosphere.

POLLUTANT. A substance not naturally found in the air, or one that is present in higher-than-normal concentrations. Pollutants can produce ill health or other undesirable effects.

PPM (PARTS PER MILLION). The number of parts of gas, by volume, in a million total parts.

PROPELLANT. A gas that sprays out the contents from pressurized containers, such as spray cans.

RADIOACTIVE. Giving off rays or particles that can penetrate plant and animal tissues. Radioactive particles can cause cellular changes in living tissue. They can also produce cancers in animals and humans.

RESIDUE. A substance left behind, such as a chemical deposit after an insecticide is sprayed.

RESPIRABLE PARTICLES. Particles (usually less than 5 microns) small enough to be inhaled into the lungs.

STANDARD. The range of minimum or maximum levels of a substance (usually an air contaminant) that has been established by a government agency as being safe for human exposure.

TOLERANCE. The ability to withstand exposure to a substance or condition without harm.

TOXIC. Able to produce negative health effects after physical contact, swallowing, or breathing in the substance.

VAPORS. The gaseous state of a substance that is usually solid or liquid at room temperature.

VENTILATION. The controlled movement of air into and out of a closed area.

VOLATILITY. The ease with which a solid or liquid changes to a gaseous form under normal atmospheric conditions of temperature and pressure.

LAWS AND AGENCIES

ACID PRECIPITATION ACT (1980). A milestone in air pollution legislation. It created a ten-year program and set up a task force to study the causes and effects of acid precipitation.

CITY ORDINANCES ON SMOKE CONTROL. Among the first laws to address the problem of air pollution. As early as 1881, both Chicago and Cincinnati had smoke control laws. By 1912, thirteen American cities with populations over 200,000 had adopted laws to control smoke.

In recent years, further pollution reductions have been achieved in most cities by: 1) prohibiting and limiting open fires for burning leaves or garbage, 2) prohibiting the use of incinerators unless they are fitted with scrubbers or filters, and 3) establishing guidelines to insure proper combustion of fuels in engines and heating systems. By the late 1970s, almost no U.S. cities exceeded the National Air Quality Standards for particulate matter or sulfur dioxide levels.

CLEAN AIR ACT. First adopted in 1963 and amended in 1965, 1970, and 1977, the several versions of this law gave the EPA authority to establish air quality standards. Periodically Congress considers amendments to the act. Clean air was defined as air with less than 20 to 40 micrograms of particulate matter per cubic meter. Guidelines were set up to check on the release of hazardous substances into the air by cars, power plants, and industry.

The 1970 Amendment set limits on six major pollutants. It also enabled the EPA to establish emission levels for new pollution sources. Amendments in 1977 altered some aspects of the act. Automobile tailpipe emissions were a major issue covered in both the 1970 and 1977 versions.

CLEAN INDOOR AIR ACTS. State laws and local ordinances that cover such issues as banning cigarette, pipe, or cigar smoking in public places. Establishing standards for allowable asbestos levels in public buildings is another similar concern.

COMPREHENSIVE ENVIRONMENTAL RESPONSE, COM-PENSATION, AND LIABILITY ACT (CERCLA) (1980). Set up the EPA Superfund for cleaning up specific pollution problems.

CONSUMER PRODUCT SAFETY COMMISSION (CPSC). Commission researchers evaluate the safety and health impact of consumer products, especially those that may emit toxic vapors (e.g., formaldehyde) or release asbestos fibers. The agency sets safety standards for products and can force hazardous items off the market. The agency also provides public information on product safety.

THE COUNCIL ON ENVIRONMENTAL QUALITY. Part of the executive branch of the federal government. It is, therefore, directly under the president's leadership. It was formed in 1969 to recommend national policies to promote improvement of the quality of the environment. It consists of three members appointed by the president with the advice and consent of the Senate.

DEPARTMENT OF AGRICULTURE. This department works to protect the environment by helping to manage soil, water, and forest resources. Community waste disposal, the safe use of pesticides, and the development of pesticide alternatives are among its responsibilities that relate to air pollution.

DEPARTMENT OF ENERGY. This department is concerned with the country's overall energy policy, especially as it relates to the impact of energy use on the environment, human safety, and health. Indoor air quality is an important concern of the department.

DEPARTMENT OF HEALTH AND HUMAN SERVICES. Major agencies under this department's leadership include:
1) Public Health Service
2) Centers for Disease Control
3) Agency for Toxic Substances and Disease Registry
4) Food and Drug Administration
5) Health Resources and Services Administration
6) National Institutes of Health
7) National Cancer Institute
8) National Heart, Lung, and Blood Institute
9) National Institute of Allergy and Infectious Diseases

DEPARTMENT OF HOUSING AND URBAN DEVELOPMENT (HUD). This government agency, which regulates standards for housing throughout the United States, is particularly concerned with the materials and methods used in home construction. HUD monitors the impact of various pollutants such as asbestos, radon, or formaldehyde (released by carpeting and building materials).

DEPARTMENT OF THE INTERIOR. The agency's environmental concern is primarily with preserving national parks and historical monuments in their original settings.

DEPARTMENT OF STATE. Includes the Bureau of Oceans and International Environmental and Scientific Affairs. The Department of State's concern with environmental issues is on a global scale.

EMERGENCY PLANNING AND COMMUNITY RIGHT-TO-KNOW ACT. Enacted in 1986, this law requires companies to inform public authorities in cases of accidents involving toxic materials. It also requires state and local groups to establish plans for handling emergencies involving toxic wastes and chemicals.

ENVIRONMENTAL PROTECTION AGENCY (EPA). Headed by a Cabinet secretary, the agency's responsibility is to study and control pollution issues. Once studies have been made, the EPA determines ways to interact with state and local governments to combat the pollution. Formed in 1970, the EPA is responsible for programs that deal with air, water, soil, radiation, solid and toxic wastes, pesticides, and noise.

MONTREAL PROTOCOL. A 1987 agreement endorsed by the United States and the governments of several industrial nations to reduce production of chlorofluorocarbons (CFCs). Plans call for cutting the production of CFCs in half by 1999. The document may serve as a model for other treaties involving international environmental issues.

MOTOR VEHICLE AIR POLLUTION CONTROL ACT (1965). Established national standards for automobile exhausts. The requirement to equip cars with catalytic converters came about as a result of this act. The act was altered again in 1967 and then replaced by the Clean Air Act of 1970.

NATIONAL AIR QUALITY STANDARDS. As part of the Clean Air Act of 1970, the U.S. government set standards for certain common atmospheric contaminants. The hazards to human health are great if an individual's exposure to them exceeds these limits more than once per year. From time to time, new standards for additional substances are established.

Primary and secondary standards exist for sulfur oxides, particulate matter, carbon monoxide, ozone, atmospheric hydrocarbons, nitrogen oxides, and lead.

The standards were established based on observations of plants, animals, and humans as well as the atmosphere itself. Primary standards are those established to protect human health. Secondary standards were established to protect against any and all adverse effects of atmospheric contaminants. These effects include damage to both living and nonliving things in the environment.

NATIONAL ENVIRONMENTAL SATELLITE DATA AND INFORMATION SERVICE. A division of the National Oceanic and Atmospheric Administration (NOAA), part of the Department of Commerce. The agency collects and interprets satellite data concerning the earth's surface and atmosphere.

NATIONAL INSTITUTE FOR OCCUPATIONAL SAFETY AND HEALTH (NIOSH). A government agency concerned with conditions in the workplace. The agency makes recommendations for limits on exposure to hazardous substances.

NATIONAL OCEANIC AND ATMOSPHERIC ADMINISTRATION (NOAA). A division of the Department of Commerce that gathers information on the earth's atmospheric and oceanic resources.

NUCLEAR REGULATORY COMMISSION. This group is concerned with the civilian uses of nuclear energy and particularly how these uses affect public health, safety, and the atmosphere.

OCCUPATIONAL SAFETY AND HEALTH ACT. Passed in 1970, the act was created to give workers safe and healthy work conditions.

The act also created the Occupational Safety and Health Administration (OSHA).

OCCUPATIONAL SAFETY AND HEALTH ADMINISTRATION (OSHA). Sets and enforces air quality standards for certain known pollutants to protect the health and safety of people in the workplace. It is part of the Department of Labor.

OFFICE OF OCEANIC AND ATMOSPHERIC RESEARCH. A division of the National Oceanic and Atmospheric Administration (NOAA), part of the Department of Commerce.

OFFICE OF SCIENCE AND TECHNOLOGY POLICY. An agency that coordinates national policy on many areas of national concern, including the economy, national security, health, foreign relations, and the environment.

RESOURCE CONSERVATION AND RECOVERY ACT. This act was passed to prevent improper dumping of harmful substances. The act designates agencies to monitor hazardous substances.

STATE IMPLEMENTATION PLANS (SIPs). The Clean Air Act required each state to develop State Implementation Plans (SIPs) to detail ways air quality standards are to be met. The method of implementation is left to each state. In 1977, amendments to the Clean Air Act extended deadlines for compliance with the original legislation.

SUPERFUND. A fund of $1.6 billion, allocated in 1980 for a five-year program to identify and clean up dump sites that are potentially hazardous to human health and safety. Under the program, more than 30,000 such sites have been identified. In 1986 the Superfund Amendments and Reauthorization Act gave the EPA more power to regulate chemicals and toxic substances. Funding was also increased to $8.5 billion.

TAILPIPE EMISSION CONTROLS. These were first legislated in the 1960s in California. Amendments to the original legislation through 1975 have decreased tailpipe emissions by more than 90 percent.

AIR TERMS

A

ACETALDEHYDE (CH3CHO). A colorless, fuming liquid with a fruitlike odor. Acetaldehyde is mildly toxic and highly flammable. It is used in industry. Hydrocarbons from smoke, smog, and automobile emissions may be changed into acetaldehyde. Long-term exposure to high concentrations of acetaldehyde can cause lung and kidney damage.

ACID DUST. Dust from smoke that contains the ingredients of acid in a dry form. These dust particles have not been exposed to atmospheric moisture to create acid rain.

Some of the hydrocarbon, sulfur, and nitrogen dioxide fumes given off by factories, home heating systems, and automobiles become acid dust. These substances are not carried away by the winds or lifted by air currents high into the atmosphere. They return as dust to earth almost immediately and very close to their place of origin. These particles are sometimes known as dry deposition. Dry deposition may damage trees and crops. Most acid dust also corrodes paint and building stonework.

ACID PRECIPITATION. The name given to rain, snow, hail, fog, mist, or sleet that has been made acidic by exposure to atmospheric smoke and fumes. Acid precipitation is caused mainly by sulfur dioxide and nitrogen oxides that enter the atmosphere during combustion of fossil fuels. These gases turn into acids when they combine with atmospheric water vapor and form acid clouds. The acid clouds can then produce "wet deposition," another name for acid rain, snow, mist, or fog.

Often winds carry the clouds that form acid precipitation many thousands of miles away from where the contamination by factory or automobile emissions occurred. As these clouds cool, the droplets they contain condense and fall as acid rain. In the springtime, acid snow melts. The water runs off into rivers and lakes. The levels of acidity in these lakes and rivers rise. Many freshwater lakes have already "died" as a result of their high acid content.

ACID RAIN. Any rainwater with a pH reading of 5.6 or less. Clouds containing sulfur and nitrogen oxides form acids as they mix with water vapor and condense. This is known as the wet deposition phase. Acid rain clouds may be carried by the wind hundreds of miles from their source. Rain that is between ten and seventy times more acid than unpolluted rain is common in much of North America and Europe. Airborne pollutants do not respect national boundaries. Disputes between Canada and the United States and among many European nations have been sparked by the acid rain problem.

Acid rain tends to be most acidic in the eastern United States. Prevailing winds out of the west carry air mixed with smokestack emissions from all across North America. Coal-fired power plants in the Midwest emit sulfur oxides. These oxides are believed to be the principal source for the acid rain that falls in the American Northeast and parts of Canada.

Acid rain directly affects many aspects of life. It can damage entire

26

forests. Trees may lose their leaves or needles and have stunted growth and abnormal bark. This weakens them and makes them more easily damaged by insects, plant diseases, and bad weather.

Acid rain runs into lakes and rivers, polluting drinking water and killing the plant and animal life in the water. It can also corrode the stone and metal of buildings and bridges.

Soil can neutralize a certain amount of the acidity that it receives as a result of acid rain. More often acid pollution washes nutrients out of the soil. It causes soil imbalances that can weaken or kill off plants and crops.

Acid lakes and rivers cause even more problems. Acid river water may flow into lakes, making them more acidic. Some fish can adapt to higher acidity—for a while—but finally only the strongest life survives. Insects and their larvae, snails, and worms near the bottom of the food chain find it particularly hard to live. Birds, too, that feed on these lower forms of life may find their food sources dwindling. Acid rain has killed the fish in hundreds of lakes in New York State's Adirondack Mountains. Canada's government claims that 14,000 lakes in the eastern part of that country have suffered damage.

Solutions to the problem of acid rain are being tested in different parts of the world. Cleaning the sulfur out of fuels before they are burned is one way. It attacks the problem of acid pollution before it can happen. Desulfurization can reduce the amount of harmful oxides by about 90 percent. But cleaning the sulfur out of fuels requires costly equipment and may produce additional waste products. However, the so-called "clean coal" technology is cheaper and more effective than the smokestack scrubber and other end-of-the-line methods now available. In these technologies, exhaust gases from factories are treated with chemicals or passed through filters. Car exhaust can be reduced by the use of catalytic converters.

At a meeting in Bulgaria in November of 1988 the United States signed a twenty-five-nation treaty. This document is designed to limit nitrogen dioxide emissions—after sulfur the principal cause of acid precipitation—and other environmental pollutants. The agreement will take effect in 1994 and will hold emissions to 1987 levels, which were already fairly high. (12, 23)

ACTIVATED CARBON (CHARCOAL). Wood heated to an extremely high temperature and then treated with pressurized steam. This processing leaves tiny holes or pores in the surface of the charcoal. Activated carbon or charcoal is used as a filtering material to remove pollutants from the air. The pores in the charcoal collect pollutants, especially gases.

AEROSOLS. Extremely fine solid or liquid particles, larger than molecules and yet too small to settle easily under the pull of gravity. Because they are so small (usually less than 1 micron), aerosols can stay suspended in the air indefinitely. Smoke and fog are examples of aerosols that occur in nature. The most common solid chemical aerosols are made up of mineral dusts, fly ash (including metal dusts), hydrocarbon particles, sodium carbonate, calcium sulfate, ammonium sulfates from industrial processes, or sodium chloride (especially from sea salt).

AEROSOL SPRAY CANS. Containers whose contents are released under pressure. A propellant gas forces the material out of the can. Aerosol spray cans have been used for a variety of household products. These products range from deodorants and oven cleaners to processed foods such as whipped cream.

Until very recently, the gases called chlorofluorocarbons (CFCs) were used as propellants. In the early 1980s, the United States (alone among the countries in which spray cans are used) placed severe restrictions on the use of CFCs as propellants. Scientists found that CFCs are damaging to the earth's ozone layer. Manufacturers have found many effective substitutes to use as propellant gases, including carbon dioxide and free nitrogen, that do not cause environmental damage. See also **CHLOROFLUOROCARBONS, HYDROCHLOROFLUOROCARBONS, OZONE HOLE,** and **OZONE LAYER.**

AGENT ORANGE. See **DIOXIN.**

AIR. A colorless, tasteless, and odorless mixture of gases made up mostly of nitrogen and oxygen. Every man, woman, and child requires about 30 pounds (13.6 kilograms) of air each day to receive enough oxygen to live and grow. Clean air is essential to health.

Standard clean air is generally considered to be made up of nitrogen (78.10%); oxygen (20.93%); argon (0.93%); hydrogen (0.01%); carbon dioxide (0.003 to 0.004%); krypton (0.0001%); neon (0.0018%); helium (0.0005%); and xenon (0.00001%).

Even a "clean" air sample will contain certain contaminants in small amounts. These include: carbon monoxide, ozone, nitrogen oxide, and nitrogen dioxide. Ozone may have come from higher atmospheric layers. Other gases may have come from organic decomposition or weather processes.

Relatively little pure air remains in the atmosphere. Air holds germs, pollen, dust, and various pollutants including waste gases from factories, smoke particles, and automobile exhaust. Air affects the inanimate world also. Exposure to air and wind affects the weathering of rocks and soils. It is one of the chief sources of building material deterioration.

Polluted air can affect human health in many ways. It has been linked to many diseases. To help protect against air contaminants, the linings of the nose and lungs secrete sticky mucus that captures some of these particles and germs. Special cells in the lungs called phagocytes attack and eat dust, germs, and other particles. Tiny moving hairs called cilia also line the breathing passages and help to expel mucus and dead phagocytes. (1, 2)

AIR CONDITIONERS. Electrical devices that cool and clean the air. However, air conditioners may add to indoor air pollution and the so-called "sick-building" syndrome. Air conditioner motors and filters are breeding grounds for bacteria, viruses, and fungal spores. Water vapor condenses on the compressor and coils inside the air conditioner. This provides a cool, damp environment where microorganisms can grow. Fans inside the equipment can spread these microorganisms throughout homes and buildings. It is therefore important that cooling systems be cleaned regularly. See also **INDOOR AIR POLLUTION** and **SICK–BUILDING SYNDROME.**

AIR FRESHENERS. See **INDOOR AIR POLLUTION.**

AIR POLLUTION. Atmospheric contamination from both natural and manmade sources. There are two kinds of atmospheric pollutants: (1) solid or liquid particles of widely varying sizes and (2) gases. Both types of pollutants may come from organic or inorganic sources.

Combustion of wood and fossil fuels accounts for about 85 percent of all manmade air pollution. Of these fuels, pollutants from automotive exhausts, industrial processes, and power plant emissions are the biggest producers of manmade pollutants. Other sources include dust, dirt, and bacteria.

Air pollution may also be created by environmental incidents or crises. A brief period of weather stagnation can cause pollutants to build to a dangerous level. Catastrophic releases of harmful substances, as at Bhopal, India, or Chernobyl, U.S.S.R., also pollute the air on a large scale. The disappearance of the ozone layer and the apparent global warming trend are examples of ongoing pollution problems.

The most immediate and serious effect of air pollution is damage to human health. Breathing polluted air can harm the lungs. Air pollution also poses problems for animals, plants, vehicles, buildings, and structures such as roads and bridges. When there is a strong wind, dirty air can be swept away and replaced with cleaner air. Mechanical and chemical control devices can also reduce the quantities of pollutants released by industry. See also **INDUSTRIAL POLLUTION** and **POLLUTION CONTROL DEVICES.**

AIR POLLUTION CONTROL. See **POLLUTION CONTROL DEVICES.**

AIR QUALITY STANDARDS. A set of objectives for limiting the levels of certain pollutants. International air quality standards were first established in 1972 by the World Health Organization (WHO), a branch of the United Nations. Many countries around the world have adopted these guidelines. They have set up standards for monitoring five major pollutants: sulfur oxides, smoke, carbon monoxide, photochemical oxidants, and nitrogen dioxide. The standards set limits for safe levels of exposure to these pollutants.

Lower concentrations of substances may be harmful too, especially after years of exposure. The fact is, no one really knows what is safe. Effects may vary widely from individual to individual.

In 1971, the United States set air quality standards for six common classes of pollutants: particulates (smoke, etc.), sulfur oxides, carbon monoxide, nitrogen dioxide, photochemical oxidants, and hydrocarbons.

AIR/SOIL EXCHANGE. Soil and dust contain particles of rock and organic debris. The action of the wind causes the erosion of rock and soil particles that end up in the atmosphere. The geography and geology of a region affect the mineral content, color, and texture of dust. Dust from North Africa's Sahara Desert is swept eastward across the continent where it gives the waters of the Red Sea their reddish tinge.

The weathering of rocks can also release chemicals, including carbonates whose breakdown contributes to total carbon dioxide levels in the atmosphere. The earth is also a source of other gases: for

31

example, radon seeping from rock particles in the soil. Volcanoes release carbon dioxide and sulfur dioxide gases from deep rock layers. Huge quantities of dust and ash are also sent into the stratosphere by the tremendous force of volcanic eruptions.

The soil is the source of various biological pollutants—soil bacteria, fungi, and molds. Soil bacteria turn nitrogen gas from the air into nitrogen compounds that plants absorb through their roots. This process releases organic and inorganic gases. Similarly, the rotting of plant and animal matter increases atmospheric levels of the greenhouse gases: carbon dioxide, nitrogen oxides, and methane and other hydrocarbons.

AIR/WATER EXCHANGE. The type and quantity of pollutants in the air directly affect the way air and ocean water exchange heat. The contents of the air affect the amount of heat from the sun that is absorbed or reflected. Particulate matter, ozone levels, and quantities of atmospheric gases all influence the amount of heat energy absorbed by the atmosphere. Heat transfer is a driving force behind weather, climate, and the formation of storms.

Earth's air currents and water currents are parts of a vast system that governs weather. Winds and waves interact. Material from the ocean provides most of the natural pollution of the atmosphere. Salt aerosols from the action of wind and wave on the sea are the largest single source of particulate matter.

Water temperatures affect the amount of dissolved gases the oceans can hold. In general, cool water can hold more dissolved gases such as oxygen or carbon dioxide. The agitation of water can release gases, such as radon or hydrogen sulfide, dissolved in it.

AIRBORNE RADIOACTIVITY. Radioactive dust or gases in the atmosphere. Airborne radioactivity is caused by nuclear fallout and by radioactive debris from the processing of radioactive ores and fuels. Tests of nuclear weapons were conducted in the atmosphere until they were banned by treaties in 1960. These tests were a source of radioactive decay products, especially strontium.

Commercial uses of nuclear fuels in power generation and in limited civil engineering projects (for blasting or excavation) are other sources of airborne radioactivity in the environment. See also **DISASTERS, POLLUTION–RELATED.** (4)

ALLERGIES. An unusual sensitivity to particular substances. Small quantities of the substance cause the body to produce special proteins called antibodies. These antibodies cause the physical symptoms of the allergy such as coughing, sneezing, or eye and breathing passage irritation.

Allergens are allergy-causing agents that are often airborne particles. Dusts; smoke; pollen; microorganisms; particles of insect, bird, or animal feces; bacteria; molds; mildews; and fungi are all potential allergens that may be airborne. Chemical pollutants in the air can also make allergies worse.

Inflammation of the nasal linings may be caused by pollen and larger particles. Molds and organic dusts can cause asthma in susceptible individuals. Smaller particles may be breathed deep into the lungs, where they can inflame lung tissues. (15)

AROMATIC HYDROCARBONS (Common abbreviation is **HC**). Complex organic chemical compounds including benzene, naphthalene, and toluene. The aromatics are among the most toxic hydrocarbons and are found in most petroleum products, including crude oil. They have become common environmental pollutants. They enter the air in exhausts from internal combustion engines. Some of the aromatics are carcinogenic.

ARSENIC (As). Arsenic is a semimetallic, silver-gray element that occurs in several chemical forms. At high temperatures it burns to form arsenic oxide, which appears as a white cloud. This is its most common form as an atmospheric pollutant.

Arsenic is used to make metal alloys, pigments, animal poisons, and insecticides. Arsenic is also used in glassmaking, taxidermy, fireworks, ammunition, and electronics.

Arsenic compounds are used in processing cotton and make cotton dust even more hazardous. Fresh fruits and vegetables are sometimes sprayed with arsenic compounds. There are many opportunities for minute particles of arsenic to enter the environment.

Arsenic is an irritant and allergic sensitizer. Arsenic has been recognized as a cause of cancers of the skin, digestive tract, and internal organs.

ART AND ANTIQUITIES, EFFECTS OF POLLUTION ON. The waste gases produced by industry and automobile traffic are damaging many of the world's most famous buildings and monuments. Rain, which cleanses the air of dust and particles, also turns the airborne gases into nitric and sulfuric acids. The acid rain reacts with limestone or marble monuments and turns their surfaces into gypsum, a soft substance that crumbles and dissolves easily.

In Athens, the Parthenon and other buildings on the Acropolis have begun to crumble because of damage from pollutants. Experts say that there has been more damage and erosion in the past twenty years from manmade pollutants than from 2,500 years of natural weathering. The monuments of Egypt, however, have fared much better. The dryness of Egypt's climate keeps down both the damage caused by acid rain and the corrosive effect of moist air.

In Paris, London, Florence, Venice, New York, and other cities around the world, massive efforts have been launched to save the heritage of open air sculpture, monuments, buildings, and even stained glass before it is too late.

New laws are being enacted that require low-sulfur content in coal and heating oil. These laws will help reduce the amount of sulfuric acid produced by sulfur oxides in the air. Correcting the damage caused by acid dust or acid rain is expensive and involves painstaking procedures. Once repairs are made, the surface of the material can be chemically sealed to prevent further damage by airborne pollutants and moisture.

The insides of art museums, too, must be protected against the harmful effects of the atmosphere. Even the breath of museum visitors carries water vapor and dusts that promote the growth of molds, fungi, and microorganisms that can damage and destroy paintings, sculpture, textiles, and other works of art. Air conditioning and filtering systems in museum buildings can help keep art treasures safe from damaging substances in the air.

ASBESTOS. A mineral fiber composed of various magnesium compounds. Because it is flexible and fireproof, asbestos has been used widely in insulating and building materials. Asbestos fibers may be bound in cement, synthetic resins, or other construction materials used in schools and public buildings. Asbestos is soundproof, and it makes concrete stronger. In the twentieth century alone, industry in the United States has used more than 30 million tons of asbestos. The EPA estimates that 2,000 to 3,000 types of manufactured goods contain asbestos. Some of these products include automotive brake linings, roofing shingles, and water pipes. In mid-1989, the EPA ordered that many asbestos products be phased out by 1997.

As asbestos ages, it disintegrates. When it is exposed, it gives off tiny airborne particles that can be inhaled. Scientists estimate that more than a half million commercial and public buildings in America contain damaged, friable (or crumbling) asbestos. It is in this friable state that asbestos is considered a threat in the air we breathe.

Pipes and ducts insulated with asbestos are still in use in many public buildings, including schools, hospitals, and homes for the aged.

If these pipes rupture, huge amounts of asbestos dust can be released.

Federal regulations require that all asbestos be removed from school buildings. In most cases this is extremely costly. In late 1988 a study released in *The New York Times* showed that about two thirds of New York City's buildings contained asbestos. Almost 90 percent of that asbestos was damaged. The study was the first such detailed analysis of the asbestos problem on a local level done in the United States. Officials said that removing asbestos from city-owned buildings alone would cost over $100 million.

Some recent studies indicate that the asbestos problem might not be as severe as had been previously thought. The controversy continues.

Asbestos particles can cause a lung disease known as asbestosis, which makes breathing difficult. In addition, cancers of the lungs, stomach, and abdominal lining have been traced to inhalation of asbestos fibers. It may take up to forty years for symptoms to develop following asbestos exposure. In many cases, victims of the disease have been workers in factories, shipyards, and other industrial sites where asbestos dust is plentiful. Studies show that 20 to 40 percent of all people have some asbestos particles in their lungs. Some reports indicate that between 8,000 and 10,000 deaths a year may be caused by asbestos-related cancers. See also **RESPIRABLE FIBERS**.

ASTHMA. A respiratory disease marked by breathing difficulty. Chest muscle contractions cause wheezing and coughing. Attacks may last from a few minutes to several days. Asthma attacks are often allergic reactions to various kinds of dust, bacterial spores, or chemical irritants in the air.

Workers in certain industries are particularly susceptible to specific types of asthma. For example, workers who inhale cotton dust may have attacks of breathlessness and coughing. See also **RESPIRABLE FIBERS**.

ATMOSPHERE. The envelope of air surrounding the earth. The atmosphere is made up of three roughly defined zones or layers: the troposphere, stratosphere, and ionosphere. Over 99 percent of the earth's atmosphere occurs within 40 to 50 miles (64 to 80 kilometers) of the earth's surface. Farther from the earth the molecules of air become more widely dispersed until the realm of space is reached.

The lowest level of the atmosphere is the troposphere. This layer includes the air in which we live and breathe. The troposphere extends upward directly from the earth's surface to a height of about 5 miles (8 kilometers) at the poles to about 7 miles (11.3 kilometers) at middle latitudes and to 10 miles (16 kilometers) at the Equator. The layer of air that plants, animals, and humans breathe is all troposphere. The troposphere is the principal atmospheric layer where air pollution problems occur. Wind and air currents, along with the earth's natural rotation, help to spread pollutants into the stratosphere.

The stratosphere is the layer of atmosphere around the earth above the troposphere. It begins about 5-1/2 miles (9 kilometers) over the earth at the Poles, from 6 to 7 miles (10 to 11 kilometers) above the earth in the middle latitudes, and 10 miles (16 kilometers) above the earth at the Equator, and extends outward about 20 miles (32 kilometers). It is a zone where the air is dry and thin, cold and clear.

The ozone layer is a part of the stratosphere about 12 to 30 miles (19 to 48 kilometers) up. This layer is where most of the sun's ultraviolet rays are intercepted. Without this "filter," the sun's radiation would destroy all animal life on the earth.

Sometimes volcanic eruptions and nuclear explosions can send dust particles into the stratosphere. Once there, high winds disperse them over a wide area. Dust here also tends to block heat energy from the sun. This keeps it from reaching the earth and thus has a cooling effect.

The ionosphere is the highest layer of the atmosphere, extending upward approximately 50 to 400 miles (80 to 640 kilometers). At the maximum distance, the ionosphere turns into the magnetosphere.

Changes in the charged particles that make up the ionosphere influence the amount of ultraviolet radiation received from the sun. See also **AIR, NUCLEAR WINTER,** and **OZONE LAYER.** (1, 2, 24)

AUTOMOBILE EXHAUST. A mixture of more than 200 chemicals, waste gases, smoke, and dust particles produced by automobile engines. These internal combustion engines are the single greatest source of manmade pollutants. They account for well over half of the total mass of pollutants expelled into the atmosphere by human activities.

The atmospheric contaminants produced by gasoline-powered cars and trucks are called tailpipe emissions. They are of four major types: 1) hydrocarbons that include uncombusted particles and partially combusted fuel vapors, 2) carbon monoxide, 3) nitrogen oxides, and 4) lead and heavy metal particles. Automobile exhaust is the principal source of lead particles in the air.

By themselves, the incompletely burned fuel vapors cause little harm as primary pollutants. However, with nitrogen oxides in the presence of sunlight they combine to form photochemical oxidants. These include ozone and the other irritating chemicals in smog.

Even with restrictions designed to reduce exhausts, it is believed that motor vehicles still account for 60 percent of the air pollutants in a large city. Car exhaust gases are usually invisible and are often harder to detect than the smoke from industrial chimneys. Even invisible, though, automobile exhausts can be a serious health threat. See also **CATALYTIC CONVERTER, HYDROCARBONS, INTERNAL COMBUSTION ENGINE,** and **LEAD.**

B

BACTERIAL POLLUTION. Airborne dust particles that contain bacteria, viruses, and other disease-causing microorganisms. They may be circulated in buildings through air conditioning, heating, and ventilation systems. Bacteria range in size from 1.0 micron to about 25 microns. See also **INDOOR AIR POLLUTION, LEGION-NAIRE'S DISEASE**, and **SICK–BUILDING SYNDROME**. (15)

BAGHOUSE. A pollution control device designed to trap dust particles. The device directs streams of gas through huge filter bags, usually made up of glass fibers. A baghouse is capable of removing up to 99.9 percent of particulate matter from polluted air. Baghouses are often fitted onto the smokestacks of factories that produce large quantities of dust. Cement production, mining operations, and metal processing industries are examples.

BENZENE (C_6H_6; also called **BENZOL** or **PHENYL HYDRIDE**). A colorless, flammable, toxic liquid with a pleasant, aromatic odor. Benzene is obtained from the distillation of coal tars. It is also a by-product in the manufacture of coke. Benzene and related hydrocarbons are used in the manufacture of plastics, synthetic rubber, dyes, and drugs.

Benzene is a common air contaminant. It is found in cleaning solvents and paint removers and also occurs in automobile exhausts. Benzene levels are 30 to 50 percent higher in the homes of smokers.

At low levels, the chemical can cause headaches, nausea, and asthma. There is evidence that long-term benzene exposure may lead to leukemia and other cancers.

BENZO(A)PYRENE ($C_{20}H_{12}$: abbreviation is **BaP**). A yellowish crystalline substance. Benzo(a)pyrene is a combustion product of fossil fuels, heating oil, natural gas, and automotive fuel, especially diesel fuel. Coal processing is the major contributor of benzo(a)pyrene to the atmosphere. Benzo(a)pyrene is found in coal tar. In the home, the level of the substance is increased by cigarette smoking and food preparation, especially broiling certain foods.

Between 1950 and 1970 major cities documented a decrease in air levels of benzo(a)pyrene, because coal is being used less and less as a heating fuel. But workers who handle asphalt, tars, coal tars, oil, and gas still face exposure to the substance. Medical studies link the chemical to lung cancer and other forms of cancer.

BERYLLIUM (Be). An extremely lightweight, silver-gray metal that is resistant to corrosion and is highly toxic. Stronger than steel and lighter than aluminum, it has many uses in the aerospace and nuclear industries. When metal ores or alloys containing beryllium are processed, tiny particles of the metal dust enter the atmosphere. Long-term exposure to high concentrations of beryllium dust may make workers ill. Victims show signs of metal poisoning, including lung and kidney damage.

BHOPAL (INDIA) DISASTER. See DISASTERS, POLLUTION–RELATED.

BIOLOGICAL POLLUTANTS. A wide range of materials from biological sources that wind up in the air as dust. These include viruses and bacteria; pollen grains; spores from molds and fungi; particles of insect and animal feces; fragments of plant and animal debris from leaves, hair, fur, and dead cells. Organic gases from the decay of dead plant and animal matter add to the pollution.

Plant metabolism releases vast quantities of organic gases. The process of digestion, particularly in ruminant animals, produces huge quantities of methane, one of the greenhouse gases linked to global warming. The action of bacteria found in rice paddies and swamps is another major source of methane. See also **GREENHOUSE GASES** and **METHANE.**

BIOSPHERE. The envelope of earth's air, water, and land. It is the realm of living things of all kinds as they interact with their environment. It includes the hydrosphere (the world of water), the lithosphere (the world of rocks and soil), and the atmosphere (the air). From the highest mountain to the lowest depths of the sea, the basic activities within the biosphere are animal respiration, metabolism, and plant photosynthesis. The chemical cycles of carbon, oxygen, nitrogen, water, minerals, and certain other key materials play major roles in biosphere ecology.

Pollutants in the air and acid rain and toxic chemicals in soil and water have upset the life cycles of many organisms all along the food chain. An increase in particles in the air, the buildup of greenhouse gases, and the thinning of the ozone layer all affect the amount of radiation absorbed from the sun. See also **GREENHOUSE EFFECT, OZONE LAYER,** and **PARTICULATE MATTER.**

BLACK/BROWN LUNG DISEASE. Lung diseases associated with workers in certain industries. Black or brown lung disease produces coughing, wheezing, lung inflammation, and, finally, damage to lung tissue that can result in death. Many coal miners develop black lung disease after breathing coal dust for many years. The black dust builds up in the lungs. Brown lung disease occurs among cotton mill workers after years of inhaling the fine dust made when cotton fiber is turned into thread and cloth.

C

CADMIUM (Cd). A silver-white metallic element used mostly in rustproof plating and in the manufacture of certain alloys. Some paint sprays contain cadmium. Aerosols from this spray carry cadmium into the air. The smelting of common industrial metal ores also releases minute particles of the metal into the atmosphere. A common air contaminant, cadmium can also enter the soil and water supply. It is sometimes found in acid rain.

The main damage from cadmium comes through inhalation of its fumes or ingestion of any minute cadmium particles. Mild cadmium poisoning may cause coughing, sweating, and other flulike symptoms. More severe cases cause lung and kidney damage and abdominal pain. Cadmium poisoning may cause lung and prostate cancer.

CAMEROON LAKE DISASTERS. See **DISASTERS, POL-LUTION–RELATED.**

CANCER. An abnormal growth of cells in the body. There are hundreds of types of cancer. Cancer may develop in any part of the body, but certain kinds of cancer are more common than others. The illness begins when the body loses control of normal cell growth. Cancerous tissue ultimately outstrips normal tissue and deprives it of nourishment. There are many studies to show that certain air pollutants affect incidences of lung, skin, and liver cancers. Some chemicals—such as hydrocarbons or methane—alter the structure of cell parts, thereby promoting cancer. See also **LUNG CANCER** and **SKIN CANCER.**

CARBON BICHLORIDE (C_2Cl_4). A clear, colorless liquid used in dry cleaning and as a fumigant. Exposure to the chemical can cause dermatitis, eye and nose irritation, and short-term drowsiness. It can damage the liver, the heart, and the kidneys. When the chemical attacks the central nervous system, it can even cause death. It is similar to carbon dichloride. See also **PERCHLOROETHYLENE.**

CARBON DIOXIDE (CO_2). An odorless, colorless gas and one of the components of the atmosphere. The level of carbon dioxide in the atmosphere appears to be rising at a rate of 0.3 percent per year. Even so, this relatively small change in the proportion of the gas in the air is having enormous impact on the atmosphere and on the earth's climate. Carbon dioxide is the principal gas cited as a cause of the so-called greenhouse effect.

Carbon dioxide is a natural product of animal respiration. It is also formed during the complete combustion of substances containing carbon. The large-scale burning of rain forests in the world's tropical areas is another source of carbon dioxide.

There are many other natural processes that release carbon dioxide into the air. These include volcanic activity and the weathering of carbon-containing rocks (limestone, marble, and gypsum), which form a large part of the environment. The natural decay of many substances also produces carbon dioxide.

At high concentrations (above 1,000 ppm) carbon dioxide may cause headaches and drowsiness. In well-ventilated places there is no danger from carbon dioxide. In confined places, such as submarines or underground basements or vaults, the amount of carbon dioxide may interfere with necessary oxygen levels. (17, 21)

CARBON DISULFIDE (CS_2; also known as **CARBON**

BISULFIDE). A liquid organic compound that is colorless, flammable, and poisonous. When mixed with impurities, it is foul-smelling. A common air pollutant, carbon disulfide enters the atmosphere through many industrial processes. It is used to make insecticides and is a common industrial solvent.

In the lower concentrations usually encountered, sulfur dioxide can cause mood swings and brain and muscle damage. In high concentrations the vapor is very toxic by ingestion, inhalation, and skin absorption. See **PERCHLOROETHYLENE.**

CARBON MONOXIDE (CO). A colorless, tasteless, and odorless gas that is formed during incomplete combustion (the burning of fuels in a low oxygen environment). Major sources of carbon monoxide pollution include automobile exhaust, fossil fuel combustion, and home kerosene heaters. Carbon monoxide is a major component of cigarette smoke. As a result, cigarette smoking increases levels of carbon monoxide indoors and inside the body.

Carbon monoxide gas is poisonous to humans and animals because it displaces oxygen. In the bloodstream, it bonds with hemoglobin over two hundred times more readily than oxygen does. (Hemoglobin is the component of blood that carries oxygen.) This reduces the blood's ability to carry oxygen.

One hour's exposure to carbon monoxide in concentrations less than 500 ppm may produce no noticeable effect. Less than an hour's exposure to concentrations of 4,000 ppm is usually fatal. Recent studies indicate that pregnant women can pass along carbon monoxide poisoning to their unborn babies.

Statistics compiled in 1989 indicate that carbon monoxide poisoning is the leading cause of death from poisoning in the United States. Sufferers exhibit flulike symptoms, including headaches, sore throat, and dizziness. In some cases poisoning causes severe chest pains. See also **INDOOR AIR POLLUTION.**

CARBON TETRACHLORIDE (CCl₄). A colorless, liquid organic compound with an odor similar to ether. A common air contaminant, carbon tetrachloride is used in many industrial processes, including the manufacture of refrigerants. Other common uses are for dry cleaning and for cleaning metals. Carbon "tet" is also used as a spot remover. The material is sometimes used as an insecticide. It is also used in certain fire extinguishers to "smother" fires. However, carbon tetrachloride reacts at high temperatures to form the poisonous gas phosgene.

Carbon tetrachloride is very toxic in high concentrations. Exposure to the chemical can cause unconsciousness and lung, liver, and kidney damage. Mild exposure can cause digestive system problems that vary from person to person. Carbon tetrachloride can be carcinogenic. It is poisonous when absorbed through the skin or when inhaled. See also **PHOSGENE.**

CATALYTIC CONVERTER. A control device that removes pollutants from automobile exhaust. Since 1975 most passenger cars sold in the United States have been fitted with catalytic converters. Their use has cut down the quantity of pollutants entering the air.

A chemical catalyst is a substance that helps cause a chemical reaction. The catalytic converter causes chemical reactions that help turn automobile exhausts into less harmful substances. Metal plates inside the converter cause these reactions to take place. Hydrocarbons, carbon monoxides, and nitrogen oxides are changed to carbon dioxide, water, and nitrogen. See also **AUTOMOBILE EXHAUST** and **INTERNAL COMBUSTION ENGINE.**

CHEMICAL RELEASE TO AIR. Chemicals released into the atmosphere are produced by both human and natural sources. Further, some chemicals enter the atmosphere accidentally, as during an industrial accident or fire. (26)

CHEMICAL WARFARE. The use of smoke, poison gases, and other toxic substances as weapons, usually during battle. Chemical weapons may injure people or damage property. Simple ingredients, such as natural gas, rubbing alcohol, and a few other basic chemicals can be combined to make a form of nerve gas. Mustard gas, a chemical used in World War I, claimed over one million lives. During the Vietnam War, the United States used Agent Orange, a defoliant, to clear vast portions of forest in Southeast Asia.

Today's concerns about chemical warfare are largely in the Third World. International laws ban the use of chemical weapons. But in many places there are no laws to prohibit their manufacture. See also **DIOXIN.**

CHERNOBYL (U.S.S.R.) DISASTER. See **DISASTERS, POL-LUTION–RELATED.**

CHLORINE (Cl_2). A yellow-green gas, liquid, or crystal, which is a common air contaminant. Each year businesses empty tons of chlorine waste left over from industrial processes into rivers and streams. There is evidence that chlorine in the upper atmosphere—about 30 miles (48 kilometers) above the earth—destroys ozone molecules that form a protective screen from the sun's ultraviolet radiation. Chlorine combines with water vapor to form hydrochloric acid (HC1).

Chlorine is very irritating to the eyes, mucus membranes, and respiratory passages. Chlorine gas and hydrochloric acid may cause chemical burns to body tissues they contact. Lung damage can result from inhalation. In a concentration as low as 3.5 ppm, chlorine can be detected by its odor. Exposures to concentrations of 50 ppm or more are hazardous for even a short term. Even a brief exposure to chlorine of 1,000 ppm may prove fatal.

CHLOROFLUOROCARBONS (or CHLORINATED FLUORO-CARBONS or CFCs). A class of volatile organic compounds used in refrigerants and plastics. They are also used for cleaning computer microchips. Chlorofluorocarbons were used in many aerosol sprays until they were banned in 1978 by the U.S. government. They are nonflammable and noncorrosive.

Chlorofluorocarbons were originally developed in the 1920s as a safe replacement for ammonia refrigerants. They are considered to be nontoxic, but a large amount in a confined space can kill by asphyxiation.

Chlorofluorocarbons are a major component of styrofoam, used in much fast-food packaging. CFCs escape into the atmosphere through leakage of refrigerants and through rupturing of the tiny bubbles that make up plastic foams. They then drift upward into the stratosphere where they break down and release chlorine gas. Chlorine gas can destroy ozone molecules.

CFCs are responsible for helping to deplete the ozone layer. Loss of the ozone layer could, many scientists believe, lead to more cases of skin cancer through increased exposure to the sun's rays. See also **AEROSOL SPRAY CANS, HYDROCHLOROFLUOROCARBONS, OZONE LAYER**, and **REFRIGERANTS.**

CHLOROFORM ($CHCl_3$; also called **TRICHLOROMETHANE**). A volatile, colorless, nonflammable liquid with a sweet taste and a pungent odor. Chloroform is produced when chlorine reacts with ethanol. In industry, it is employed as a solvent for fats, alkaloids, and iodine. When chloroform is exposed to sun and air, it reacts to form phosgene, a poisonous gas.

Chloroform was once used as a general anesthetic during surgery. It has been replaced by safer, less toxic substances. Chloroform exposure can irritate the mucous membranes. It also affects eyesight and can cause paralysis and respiratory and cardiac arrest after prolonged inhalation. Chloroform may damage the heart, liver, and kidneys and is a suspected carcinogen.

CLIMATE CHANGE. An observable change in the world's weather patterns. Research scientists and meteorologists from all over the world have tried to explain these trends and determine their long-range effects.

The rise in the level of carbon dioxide is considered the most important factor in climate change. Carbon dioxide in the atmosphere absorbs infrared rays and keeps them from being reflected back into space.

Some scientists feel that warming trends will raise average global temperatures 3 to 4 degrees centigrade over the next fifty years. In most temperate zone areas this will triple the number of days over 90 degrees Fahrenheit. Temperatures have increased 1 degree Fahrenheit in the twentieth century already. Ocean levels will rise, flooding coastal areas. Global warming may also cause more powerful hurricanes and storms. The greatest warming changes will probably be seen in the polar regions. Northerly countries such as Canada and the U.S.S.R. will probably have warmer climates in the next century. Northern Europe will have heavier rains, especially in the winter. And it will probably be drier in the Middle East, the American Midwest and West, and North Africa.

Climate change is one of the most discussed science topics in the late twentieth century. Many scientists believe that controlling air pollution can help counteract the problems of climate change. See also **CHLOROFLUOROCARBONS, GLOBAL WARMING,** and **GREENHOUSE EFFECT.** (3, 6, 11, 16, 17, 28, 31)

CLOUDS. Tiny droplets of condensed water vapor that are suspended in the atmosphere. Clouds produce rain, snow, and other types of precipitation. Whatever is in the atmosphere—dust or chemical pollutants—ends up in the tiny water droplets that form clouds. Clouds are therefore the means by which many contaminants reach the earth's surface, especially in the form of acid precipitation.

There are many types of clouds at different levels in the atmosphere. They all have an impact on climate. Mid-level clouds are usually dense and puffy white. They reflect sunlight back into space and have a general cooling effect on the earth. Wispy high altitude cirrus clouds hold some radiant energy in the atmosphere and contribute to atmospheric warming. In general, more cloud cover means warmer temperatures.

Weather stations around the world monitor clouds in the atmosphere. Satellite information and ground measurements are studied. Radiometers measure the heat coming from the sun and the amount reflected back by the cloud cover. Scientists use this information to predict global temperatures and to track warming or cooling trends. See also **CONDENSATION NUCLEI.**

COAL. A fossil fuel made up primarily of carbon mixed with varying amounts of mineral matter. It is an important fuel because it is so plentiful. Burning coal produces soot and releases other atmospheric contaminants.

The grades of coal vary from soft to hard. The softest coal is the least valuable. Soft coal has the highest moisture content, the most impurities, and the greatest amount of volatile gases. Anthracite, or hard coal, is almost pure carbon and is very hard, black, and lustrous.

The lower grades of coal have large amounts of sulfur compounds that produce sulfur dioxide and minerals such as metals that become part of fly ash. The smoke and dust pollutants produced by soft coal equal about 10 percent of the fuel's weight. There are processes that can reduce the sulfur content of coal and produce a cleaner fuel that causes less pollution. See also **BLACK/BROWN LUNG DISEASE** and **KILLER (LONDON) FOGS.**

CONDENSATION NUCLEI. Tiny particles of smoke, soot, dust, and ash. Their sizes range from 0.1 to 10 microns, and they play a part in cloud formation. Water vapor condenses around these particles to form a mist. The mist then becomes fog if it occurs near the ground or cloud if it occurs above the ground. The cloud or fog may develop characteristics such as odor, color, or acidity, depending on the chemical nature of the particles. See also **CLOUDS.**

COPPER (Cu). A reddish metal that is a common air pollutant. It occurs in dust that comes from industrial processes and from the weathering of copper building materials or from rocks containing copper. Some copper compounds (such as copper sulfate) are used in making fungicides, insecticides, batteries, and paint. Along with other metals, small amounts of copper may occur in fuels. When fuels are burned, minute particles of metal dust enter the atmosphere. Copper is irritating to the eyes, mucous membranes, and respiratory tract.

CREOSOTE. A volatile, heavy, colorless, and oily liquid with a smoky odor. It is a mixture of hydrocarbon substances and is a common air pollutant. Tiny aerosols of creosote enter the air in smoke whenever wood or coal are burned. Creosote from coal tar sources is poisonous. Airborne creosote builds up inside chimneys of wood-burning stoves, fireplaces, and furnaces. It leaves sticky, flammable deposits that can cause chimney fires.

Creosote is an irritant and a recognized carcinogen. It causes cancers of the skin, neck, face, lungs, throat, and breathing passages.

CYCLOHEXANE (C_6H_{12}). A colorless liquid hydrocarbon with a pungent odor. It is a common air pollutant because it is a component of automobile exhaust. The chemical may be a carcinogen.

D

DEFORESTATION. See **RAIN FORESTS.**

DIOXIN. The common name for tetrachlorodibenzo-paradioxin (also known as TCDD). There are over seventy-five chemical compounds that are known as dioxins. TCDD is the most common and the most poisonous.

Dioxin is a by-product of chemical manufacture and is used to make herbicides. The herbicide Agent Orange, used in the Vietnam War, is a kind of dioxin. Some soldiers and civilians who were exposed to the defoliant are now experiencing health problems, including cancer.

Dioxin is found in some paints, varnishes, adhesives, and soaps, and in the disinfectant known as hexochlorophene. Minute quantities of dioxin contaminate most paper products as a result of their bleaching and processing. Dioxin also enters the air when industrial wastes are burned. People and animals who live near incinerators may be taking in a dangerous level of airborne dioxin produced by the burning of certain plastic wastes.

Dioxin is one of the most dangerous chemical pollutants in the atmosphere. Prolonged exposure to dioxin can result in aches and pains of muscles, nervous and psychiatric conditions, and severe acne. Laboratory animals exposed to dioxin have developed various types of cancer. Most doctors assume that humans are similarly affected, although studies of this issue continue. (14)

DISASTERS, POLLUTION–RELATED. In December of 1930, the Meuse Valley, near Liège, Belgium, was the site of one of history's first large-scale pollution-related disasters. A temperature inversion caused a thick smoke blanket of industrial gases to accumulate throughout the valley, where it remained for three days. Several thousand people became sick with respiratory troubles, and sixty people died. In 1948 similar conditions developed in Donora, Pennsylvania, when twenty people died, and some 6,000 became ill.

Three Mile Island, on the Susquehanna River in central Pennsylvania, is the site of a nuclear power station. The most serious accident to date in the history of American nuclear power occurred there on March 28, 1979.

During the accident a plume of airborne radiation was released. Winds dispersed small amounts of the radioactive gases to the northwest, northeast, and southeast. During a seven-day period developments at the site were closely monitored. Humans and animals in the vicinity of the stations received some low-level radiation exposure. Some scientists insist that the exposure was only slightly in excess of the normal background radiation received by residents of the area. Studies have linked the incident to higher than normal rates of cancer, birth defects, and miscarriages among area residents.

On the night of December 4, 1984, a toxic cloud of more than five tons of methyl isocyanate vapor was accidentally released from the Union Carbide chemical plant in Bhopal, India. After breathing the gas, more than 2,000 people died and some 200,000 were injured, many of them severely. Tens of thousands of cases of permanent blindness, sterility, and brain damage, as well as chronic kidney and liver disease, resulted from the chemical leak. Death rates among the survivors of the disaster continue to be higher than average.

The tiny African republic of Cameroon has been the site of two natural pollution-related disasters. These have occurred at lakes situated in volcanic craters. The first incident took place in 1984 at

Lake Manoum, where an eruption of cyanide gas killed thirty-seven people. The second disaster took place on the shore of Cameroon's Lake Nio in August of 1986. Seventeen hundred people died as they slept. Thousands of head of cattle and other animals were killed, and hundreds of people were injured. Deadly fumes of an unknown combination of gases exploded from the lake waters, killing both people and animals. The fumes probably included a mixture of carbon monoxide, carbon dioxide, and hydrogen sulfide or cyanide.

Some scientists think that an earth tremor caused a crack in the lake bed. The crack then freed volcanic gases that exploded from the lake. Others believe that molten rock in a shaft of the volcano under the lake warmed pockets of gases that had collected there, causing them to expand and explode.

On April 26, 1986, one of four reactors at a nuclear power station at Chernobyl in the Soviet Ukraine exploded. Superheated fuel combined with coolant water in the core of the reactor. This produced massive amounts of steam that tore the top off the reactor.

As a result of the accident, radioactive debris was released and scattered by winds over much of Europe. High levels of radioactive fallout from the blast were found in Sweden. In neighboring Poland, pregnant women were advised not to drink milk or eat fresh vegetables, which might be tainted. Food grown in areas contaminated by the accident had to be destroyed.

Over 75,000 people were evacuated from the immediate vicinity of the reactor. Within a few months of the explosion some 30 people had died as a result of the accident. Many more may die in future years from cancers caused by the high doses of radiation.

DRY CLEANING. The process of cleaning fabrics with a liquid mixture of detergent and solvents. Perchloroethylene is the solvent most commonly used. If items are not dried and aired properly after dry cleaning, they may still contain large amounts of solvent. When brought into the home, these items may be a major source of indoor pollution. Personnel who work in dry cleaning stores are also at risk from prolonged inhalation of perchloroethylene vapors. See also **INDOOR AIR POLLUTION** and **PERCHLOROETHYLENE.** (10, 15)

DUST. Small particles of almost any solid substance. Included in dust are sand and salt from the action of wind and waves on the ocean; soil and mineral particles, including silicates and carbonates, from the weathering of rock; rubber from car and truck tires; and tiny bits of cement, gravel, and asphalt from road surfaces. Particles of metals from smelting operations and rusts and other corrosion products are common components of dusts. Chemical pollutants sometimes "hitch a ride" on dust particles and are carried into the breathing passages and lungs.

Household dust can come from such everyday items as clothing and bedding, furniture, curtains, carpets, and upholstery. It contains organic and inorganic substances, chemicals from pesticides and detergents, pollen, mites, bacteria, viruses, asbestos fibers, and other particles from the air. House dust varies in composition from place to place and according to the season of the year.

Dust particles can produce growths of fibrous tissue in the lungs. These growths can obstruct breathing and promote other infections. Wood dust inhaled by sawmill workers, carpenters, and cabinetmakers has been linked to the development of cancers in the nasal passages, lungs, colon, and brain.

Dust is a factor in global temperatures and weather. It reflects sunshine and radiates heat into space. Large quantities of dust in the atmosphere (from volcanoes or from meteors striking the earth) may have led to the global cooling that helped produce the Ice Ages. See also **PARTICULATE MATTER.**

E

EL NIÑO/LA NIÑA. El Niño is a pattern of warming of water currents and air temperatures. It occurs in parts of the southern Pacific Ocean. The pattern seems to repeat every five to seven years. The name comes from Spanish and means "the boy infant"—a reference to the Christ Child, since the warming trend is often observed during the Christmas season. Research indicates that El Niño may begin deep under the sea, where volcanic eruptions heat water near the ocean floor. Warmer currents upset global weather patterns, causing droughts, flooding, and tropical storms.

In 1988, a companion phenomenon, named La Niña ("the girl infant"), was observed by scientists. Unlike El Niño, the new trend seems to be responsible for bringing colder than usual temperatures to the eastern Pacific Ocean region. La Niña may thus help offset atmospheric warming trends. The cooler ocean waters may also absorb some of the excess carbon dioxide from the atmosphere. See also **CARBON DIOXIDE** and **CLIMATE CHANGE**.

EMISSION CONTROL. See **POLLUTION CONTROL DEVICES**.

ENERGY CRISIS. A period of skyrocketing fuel prices and uncertain fuel supplies. It was sparked in 1973 by a U.S. government embargo on Arab oil imports, as well as a fear of dwindling fuel supplies.

The Energy Crisis had a mixed impact on air pollution. It promoted cutbacks in fuel use and the development of more efficient automobiles. Alternative energy schemes were also proposed. These included solar and wind power, harnessing tides, and the movement of ice floes.

But the Energy Crisis also made the air dirtier. Poorer grades of fuels, such as soft coal and high-sulfur fuel oils, generated higher levels of pollutants. In order not to waste fuel, consumers made their homes airtight. These measures, however, actually helped to seal in many types of pollutants in homes and office buildings. See also **INDOOR AIR POLLUTION.**

ENVIRONMENTAL ILLNESS. An extreme allergic reaction or sensitivity characterized by headaches, nausea, respiratory problems, rashes, swelling, and other symptoms. It is triggered by exposure to high levels of synthetic particles and chemical vapors in the environment. One of the common chemicals linked to environmental illness is formaldehyde.

Treating the illness involves isolating sufferers in a rural setting with lots of fresh air. People suffering from this disease should live in homes built and furnished only with natural materials such as untreated wood and stone. Products made from plastics must be removed from their environment. People should wear only natural fibers and should wash these clothes in pure water with nonallergenic soaps. To keep exposure to chemicals down to a minimum, people should avoid detergents, perfumes, and cosmetics. Sufferers of environmental illness must only read newspapers or other printed materials that have been aired for several days. This airing allows fumes from ink and paper processing to disperse. See also **FORMALDEHYDE** and **INDOOR AIR POLLUTION.**

F

FALLOUT. See **NUCLEAR FALLOUT.**

FLUORIDES. Compounds that contain fluorine (F). They are common air pollutants and come from many industrial sources. Fluoride gas and particles are produced by fertilizer manufacturing plants, copper smelting operations, and oil refineries. Sodium and calcium fluorides are industrial wastes. These fluorides come mostly from the making of steel, ceramic, and aluminum products.

When fluoride dust settles on food eaten by livestock, it may injure them or make them ill. Hydrogen fluoride is probably the most hazardous fluoride to human health. It is also the air pollutant most harmful to plants. Fluoride poisoning, or fluorosis, may affect the bones, teeth, and ligaments. The stannous fluoride found in many toothpastes is generally considered safe.

FLUOROCARBONS. Compounds of fluorine and carbon. In addition to chlorofluorocarbons, they have been used as aerosol spray can propellants. The fluorocarbons damage the atmosphere by helping decrease the amount of ozone. Because of this hazard, alternative propellants are now in use. These include squeeze and "pump" bottles, roll-on applicators, and spray cans that use the so-called "safe" aerosol propellant gases. See also **AEROSOL SPRAY CANS, CHLOROFLUOROCARBONS,** and **HYDRO-CHLOROFLUOROCARBONS.**

FLY ASH. Fine solid particles in smoke, especially from coal fires. It consists of material that will not burn, left over from the combustion of fossil fuels. Fossil fuels contain small amounts of rock, minerals, and metal particles such as aluminum chloride. Other sources of fly ash in the air include wood fires, charred paper or fabric, dust, cinders, and soot. Smoke from burning any of these substances always contains some traces of uncombusted material. Chemical impurities in the burning material may also be present in the particles of fly ash.

FOG. Condensed water vapor in droplets. The droplets must be small enough to remain suspended in the atmosphere. Fog is the same as a cloud that forms at ground level. The amount of water vapor and the air temperature together determine how dense the fog is.

The moisture in fog can turn oxides of nitrogen and sulfur in the air into harmful acids. In stagnant air, these acids may be very harmful to plants or building materials. Artificial fogs, made of atomized particles of oil, are used in agriculture to keep pesticides suspended.

FORMALDEHYDE (HCHO; also known as **FORMALIN, FORMOL, METHANOL,** or **FORMIC ALDEHYDE**). A clear gas or liquid with a pungent odor. It is one of the most common air pollutants, especially indoors. Most commercial formaldehyde is a solution in water that contains no more than 50 percent of the chemical mixed with methanol. Formaldehyde in a water solution is known as formalin. It is an embalming fluid.

Formaldehyde forms in nature when wood and fuels are burned. However, manmade products that outgas formaldehyde vapors are a principal source of air pollution in the human environment. Formaldehyde is often used in carpet backing, draperies, upholstery, furniture, and synthetic clothing fibers. Sometimes it is used to stiffen fabrics. It is used in the manufacture of plywood, fiber board, particle board, and other building and decorating materials.

Mobile home interiors are constructed almost entirely from fiber board and thus have a high formaldehyde content. Formaldehyde urea foam is especially controversial. The foam has been widely used in making insulation and seat cushions. It is one of the main sources of indoor air pollution. If it burns, it produces smoke that is highly toxic. Consumer groups would like to reduce the amount of formaldehyde used in building materials.

Formaldehyde is an irritant that affects mucous membranes, the eyes, skin, nose, and upper respiratory system. It can trigger asthma and lung disorders, and it is carcinogenic. Even low-level exposures to formaldehyde have produced cancer in laboratory animals. See also **ENVIRONMENTAL ILLNESS, INDOOR AIR POLLUTION,** and **SICK–BUILDING SYNDROME.**

FOSSIL FUELS. Fuels, such as coal, oil, and natural gas, formed from the remains of ancient plant and animal life. They are highly concentrated hydrocarbons that burn easily and produce heat. Complete combustion of these fuels would release only heat energy, water vapor, and carbon dioxide. However, perfect, or complete, combustion never takes place. The level of oxygen is never ideal, and carbon monoxide forms. Soft coal produces more than 10 percent of its weight in smoke, dust, and chemical pollutants.

Uncombusted material enters the atmosphere as smoke, dust, soot, and particles of tarry hydrocarbon substances. Small quantities of metal and mineral impurities are released into the air as fly ash. Sulfurous impurities produce sulfur oxides, especially sulfur dioxide. Sulfur dioxide combines with water in the air to form sulfuric acid, the largest component of acid rain. See also **COAL** and **FLY ASH.**

FREON. See **TRICHLOROTRIFLUOROETHANE.**

FUMES. The smallest kind of particles found in dust. They consist of particles that range in size from 0.001 to 1 micron. Most smoke is made up largely of fumes. Volatile liquids, including many of the hydrocarbons, are another source. Because fumes are small, they are easily inhaled deep into the lungs and are therefore a health hazard.

FUNGAL POLLUTION. Contamination by dust containing spores and/or particles of molds, mildews, and other fungi. Fungi are simple plants that lack the chlorophyll and system of veins found in more highly developed plants. Fungal spores are an example of pollution from a natural source.

Fungal spores are common indoor pollutants. They can be spread by air conditioners, humidifiers, and ventilating systems. Damp walls, cellar areas, and refrigerators provide ideal conditions for fungi to grow. Fungal pollutants can infect sinuses and cause allergic reactions. Hypersensitivity pneumonitis is a serious lung inflammation caused by spores that lodge in respiratory passages.

Little can be done to control fungal pollution outdoors. Indoors, however, good air circulation, cleanliness, and frequently changed air filters can help reduce problems caused by fungal spores. See also **BIOLOGICAL POLLUTANTS** and **INDOOR AIR POLLUTION.** (15)

FURAN (C_4H_4O; also known as **TETROL, FURFURANE,** or **FURANE**). A colorless, flammable liquid that turns brown when exposed to the air. Furan itself is the principal member of a group of related compounds called furans or furanes. It can be made by distilling wood oils from pines or from chemicals. Furan is used in the manufacture of nylon.

Plastic products that contain polychlorinated biphenyls (PCBs) can produce furan if they are burned at relatively low temperatures. Internal combustion engines are another source of furan in the atmosphere. Furan is highly toxic, whether it is ingested, inhaled, or absorbed through the skin. See also **INCINERATION** and **POLYCHLORINATED BIPHENYLS.**

G

GASOLINE. A fuel made from crude oil and used in internal combustion engines. Gasoline is highly flammable and explosive because it is made up of volatile hydrocarbons. Gasoline is a mixture of hydrocarbons that have different properties. They vaporize at different rates and burn at different temperatures. They produce varying amounts of pollutants. Sulfur oxides from impurities and lead particles from fuel additives are common pollutants produced by gasoline combustion. See also **AUTOMOBILE EXHAUST** and **INTERNAL COMBUSTION ENGINE.**

GLOBAL WARMING. The trend that seems to indicate that the earth's average temperatures are gradually rising. Scientists link this trend to air pollution and the gradual destruction of the ozone layer. The use of fossil fuels is causing an increase in the level of carbon dioxide and other gases in the atmosphere. These gases trap heat energy coming from the sun in the so-called greenhouse effect. Other gases involved include methane, nitrous oxide, and chlorofluorocarbons (CFCs).

Some consequences of the warming trend include increased melting of the polar ice caps; the rising of ocean levels; flooding of cities, harbors, and low-lying areas; and shifts in the formation of seacoasts due to encroaching water.

Along with the warming have come changes in rain and weather patterns. Drought conditions in the summer of 1988 were the worst since the Dust Bowl years of 1934–36. Global warming may cause a recurring drought in the middle of North America. At the same time rain patterns may shift farther to the north. Temperatures during the 1980s have averaged nearly 0.5 degrees Celsius higher than the average for the previous thirty years.

There is some disagreement, but European scientists assert that world temperatures have risen by 1 degree Fahrenheit since the turn of the century. Clearly the 1980s experienced some of the highest temperatures on record.

The United Nations has called for a World Environmental Policy. Elements of the policy would be the banning of industrial chemicals that deplete the ozone layer and stricter fuel-economy standards to lower consumption of gasoline. Reduced fuel consumption would keep carbon dioxide emissions down. The United Nations Environmental Program hopes to formulate an international treaty on global warming. See also **CLIMATE CHANGE, GREENHOUSE EFFECT,** and **OZONE LAYER.** (3, 6, 11, 16, 17, 28, 31)

GRAVITY SETTLERS. See POLLUTION CONTROL DEVICES.

GREENHOUSE EFFECT. The accumulation of waste gases that absorb and trap heat in the atmosphere. The heat would otherwise be reflected and dispersed into space. The greenhouse gases are chiefly carbon dioxide and chlorofluorocarbons. These gases absorb infrared radiation. Other greenhouse gases are nitrous oxides from fertilizers and automobile exhaust, and methane from bacteria in rice paddies, marshes, garbage dumps, and other agricultural sources.

Scientists make the following recommendations for slowing the effect: 1) approval and implementation of the Montreal Protocol; 2) improved energy efficiency and development of nonfossil fuel sources; and 3) cutbacks on deforestation and attempts to replant forests in parts of the world. Some scientists predict that unless we take action, levels of carbon dioxide from burning fuels will double in the next fifty years. See also **CARBON DIOXIDE, CLIMATE CHANGE,** and **GLOBAL WARMING.** (3, 16, 17)

GREENHOUSE GASES. Four common gases that scientists believe are causing the greenhouse effect. Carbon dioxide seems to account for about half the problem of global warming. The other major gases include chlorofluorocarbons (CFCs), nitrogen oxides, and methane. The heat-trapping properties of the gases act like the glass walls and ceilings in a greenhouse. Already the concentrations of these gases in the atmosphere have shown an increase. Scientists predict that average global temperatures may rise several degrees Fahrenheit within the next half century. They say that this will happen even if the amounts of the greenhouse gases stay at their present levels. See also **CLIMATE CHANGE, GLOBAL WARMING,** and **GREENHOUSE EFFECT.**

H

HALONS. A class of compounds also known as halogenated hydrocarbons. They are similar to hydrocarbons with the addition of an atom of fluorine, chlorine, bromine, or iodine. Among the more common are chloromethane and carbon tetrachloride (both solvents); chloroform and chlorobenzene; paradichlorobenzene (or moth crystals); and perchloroethylene (a popular dry cleaning solvent). Some fire-extinguishing foams are made from halons.

In concentration or after long exposure, halons are highly toxic. When they burn they produce toxic by-products that include compounds of chlorine, bromine, and fluorine. Recent studies show that certain halons are even more destructive of atmospheric ozone than chlorofluorocarbons. In particular, halons that contain bromine may destroy more ozone than chlorine compounds.

HAZARDOUS WASTES. Toxic chemicals and radioactive materials that are the by-products of many industrial processes. Disposing of the millions of tons of wastes generated each year has become a major problem. Industry often dumps the wastes or incinerates them improperly, thereby increasing pollutants in the atmosphere, ground, and water. (35, 37)

HAZE. The dirty air that hangs over urban areas. It blocks off light and reduces visibility. Yellowish haze is largely caused by sulfur oxides. Hydrocarbon emissions from fuels combine with nitrogen oxide to produce photochemical oxidants that cause grayish haze. The blue haze often seen over forests and mountains is usually produced by hydrocarbon gases that trees, especially evergreens, release to the air in hot weather. Haze may trigger asthma attacks and other respiratory troubles.

HEAT. See **THERMAL POLLUTION.**

HEAT TRANSFER. See **THERMAL POLLUTION.**

HEAVY METALS. Elements with high molecular weight that include mercury, chromium, beryllium, cadmium, arsenic, and lead. Small amounts of the heavy metals are present as impurities in many fuels. Particles of the metals are released into the air as fly ash when the fuels are burned. They are generally toxic to plants and animals. Lead is the most common metallic waste in the environment. It builds up in body tissues as a result of inhalation or ingestion of metal particles. In the body it can cause damage to the central nervous system and to internal organs.

HUMIDIFIERS. Devices designed to add moisture to heated indoor air. Dry air can irritate mucous membranes in the nose and throat.

Humidifiers may be a health risk. Sometimes a pinkish or white slime or dust is found in rooms where the humidifiers are used. This debris dispersed by the humidifier may include lead, zinc, aluminum, and asbestos dust as well as organic products and gases.

Humidifiers usually have reservoirs that hold the liquid they spray into the air. The water that stands in these reservoirs often contains microorganisms, bacteria, amoebae, viruses, and spores of molds and fungi. These pollutants are then spread by the humidifier. Many people develop allergies or other diseases when they inhale air that contains these biological pollutants. Colds, flu, and a general feverish condition called "humidifier lung" are spread in this way. More serious diseases,

such as Legionnaire's Disease, may also be spread. See also
BIOLOGICAL POLLUTANTS. (15)

HYDRIDES. A class of chemical compounds that contain hydrogen and
another element. Hydrides react violently with water to form hydrogen
and bases. Water should never be used in fires involving hydrides or to
clean up hydride chemical spills. Some hydride compounds form highly
toxic gases. These include the common atmospheric contaminants
ammonia, hydrogen sulfide, and phosphine. Ammonia is a particularly
common atmospheric pollutant. It is produced in nature by the decay of
plant and animal matter. And it is a chemical used in many industrial
processes as well as in home cleaning products.

Air that contains aerosols of hydrides can cause severe
chemical burns to eyes, mucous membranes, lungs, and breathing
passages.

HYDROCARBONS (General formula CxHy, or HC). A large class
of organic compounds that contain only hydrogen and carbon in
varying combinations. Many of them form chained, branched, or
ring-shaped molecules. Methane, the major component of natural
gas, is one of the most common hydrocarbons. Some hydrocarbons
are formed naturally in the atmosphere. Automotive and
transportation exhausts are the principal sources of manmade
hydrocarbon emissions. Industrial processes are the other important
source of hydrocarbon pollutants. The level of hydrocarbon
emissions determines the seriousness of photochemical smog.
Hydrocarbons kill plants. They are common air pollutants, and
many are carcinogenic.

HYDROCHLOROFLUOROCARBONS (HCFCs). A class of
chlorofluorocarbons with an extra hydrogen atom. The hydrogen
causes them to break down more easily. They are considered an
alternative to chlorofluorocarbons (CFCs) that destroy atmospheric

ozone. One common type, Hydrochlorofluorocarbon 22, has been used as a coolant in air conditioning units for decades. It destroys only one-twentieth the amount of ozone that an equal amount of chlorofluorocarbon would destroy. Hydrochlorofluorocarbons can also be used in making polystyrene and polyurethane foam insulation packing and stuffing materials. Other compounds are being tested that contain no chlorine. These are called hydrofluorocarbons, or HFCs. It is believed that HCFCs and HFCs could be used in place of about 60 percent of the chlorofluorocarbons now in use. See also **AEROSOL SPRAY CANS** and **CHLOROFLUOROCARBONS.**

HYDROGEN (H). A gaseous chemical element and one of the components of the atmosphere. It is the simplest element and contains a single neutron and a single electron. It is one of the main components of the molecules that make up the matter of the universe. Hydrogen reacts with many other substances and, when combined with oxygen, forms water. When chemically combined with carbon, hydrogen forms hydrocarbons and carbohydrates, as well as organic acids and bases.

HYDROGEN CHLORIDE (HCl). A colorless gas or fuming liquid with an unpleasant odor. It is corrosive and extremely poisonous. Due to its widespread use in industry, it is a common air contaminant. It can also be prepared commercially by the reaction of sulfuric acid with sodium chloride and other chemicals. Most hydrogen chloride is dissolved in water to form hydrochloric acid. Hydrochloric acid is used in metal cleaning, food processing, and in the manufacture of other chemicals. Sometimes it occurs as a by-product of the manufacture of chlorinated chemicals.

A brief exposure to 35 ppm causes throat irritation. Concentrations of 50 to 100 ppm are tolerable for periods of about an hour. Serious lung irritation and spasms result from more severe exposures.

Concentrations over 1,000 ppm are very dangerous for even a brief period of time.

HYDROGEN CYANIDE (HCN; also called **PRUSSIC ACID**). A colorless, poisonous chemical compound that has a sweet, almond-like smell. Hydrogen cyanide is emitted as an exhaust gas when coke is made from coal. In nature, hydrogen cyanide forms when ammonia and carbon monoxide combine. It may also be formed by the mixing of ammonia, oxygen, and natural gas. Hydrogen cyanide is an important insecticide and is used in the manufacture of other chemicals. It has become a major air pollutant.

Hydrogen cyanide makes body cells unable to absorb oxygen and thus causes death by asphyxiation. Exposure to concentrations of 100 to 200 ppm for half an hour to an hour can be fatal. In lesser doses the substance can cause dizziness, headache, and nausea.

HYDROGEN FLUORIDE (HF). A chemical compound that can be either a liquid or a colorless gas. Hydrofluoric acid is a water solution of hydrogen fluoride and is one of the components of acid rain.

Hydrogen fluoride is used in making fluorocarbons, and aluminum fluoride in aluminum refining. It is also used in refining nuclear fuels from uranium and in producing stainless steel.

At high concentrations, hydrogen fluoride is especially harmful to all types of trees and crops. Hydrogen fluoride is extremely irritating and corrosive to skin, mucous membranes, and respiratory passages. It produces burns to the skin that may be slow to heal.

HYDROGEN SULFIDE (H_2S). A colorless, flammable gas known as rotten egg gas because of its unpleasant odor. Dissolved in water, hydrogen sulfide forms hydrosulfuric acid. The substance is found in nature in volcanic gases and in some mineral waters. It is also produced by the bacteria that cause biological decay. Hydrogen sulfide is often a by-product of the burning of sulfur-containing fuels such as natural gas, crude oil, and coal. It is a common air contaminant.

At high concentrations, hydrogen sulfide is very poisonous. Low doses bring eye and nasal passage irritation. It can also cause corrosive damage to moist body tissues, such as those that line the lungs and breathing passages. Hydrogen sulfide can kill by leading to paralysis of the lungs.

I

INCINERATION. The burning of refuse in the presence of heat and oxygen (air). Many toxic materials can be burned by incineration to produce relatively harmless by-products. Heating to 650° C (1200° F) is effective to oxidize most waste products and to eliminate odors. Some materials require incineration at higher temperatures to destroy harmful intermediate products. These include the highly toxic dioxins and furans produced when various plastics are burned at too low a temperature. Generally, the only substances that resist incineration are the oxides of heavy metal contaminants, including lead, mercury, and cadmium. These metals may end up in fly ash that can be collected by filter devices.

The end products of incineration include carbon monoxide, carbon dioxide, water vapor, oxides of nitrogen and sulfur, aldehydes, and hydrocarbon gases. There is always a residue of particulate matter comprised of metal or mineral oxides, unburned carbon, and uncombusted refuse. Emission control devices such as smokestack filters, fly ash collectors, wet scrubbers, and electrostatic precipitators can prevent most of these wastes from entering the atmosphere. Air pollution regulations have played a large part in cleaning up incinerator emissions.

INDOOR AIR POLLUTION. The contamination of indoor air caused by pollutants from a number of sources. It is a problem in homes,

70

offices, schools, factories, businesses, and in public buildings and transportation facilities. Most people spend about 90 percent of their time indoors. Their exposure to indoor pollutants is therefore great.

Today's indoor pollution comes from building materials, insulation, cleaning products, tobacco smoke, air conditioners, furnaces and stoves, home fireplaces, appliances, and even contaminated water and food. Chemical air fresheners can actually make indoor air less clean.

Although it may seem clean, indoor air in many homes and offices can be polluted with anywhere from 100 to 250 volatile organic compounds. Many of these indoor pollutants are virtually odorless and tasteless, and most people are totally unaware of their presence. However, pollution levels are sometimes two to five times higher indoors than out. Efforts to insulate and weatherize homes and buildings have tended to trap pollutants indoors.

One of the most common sources of indoor contaminants is house dust. House dust may include dust and ash from outdoors, microorganisms, animal danders, insect excreta, and many other substances, including asbestos fibers from deteriorating floor or ceiling tiles and pipe insulation.

Garages that are adjacent to living quarters may be a source of gasoline fuel vapors, hydrocarbon soot, carbon monoxide, and other waste gases and particles associated with automobile exhausts. Leaky and defective engine parts may considerably increase the risk. Many of these common indoor pollutants are carcinogenic.

Building and decorating materials (fabrics, furniture, and carpeting) may give off toxic fumes, especially formaldehyde. Formaldehyde vapors escape from plywood, insulation, and furniture veneers, stuffing materials, or airplane seats. Pressure-treated lumber also emits toxic fumes.

According to OSHA standards, an indoor kerosene heater can produce the same hazardous levels of carbon monoxide in the home that would keep a coal miner from even entering a mine. Burned foods can release high levels of nitrogen compounds. Gas stoves in kitchens can produce nitrous oxide waste gases. Household cleaners and waxes emit organic chemicals. And the use of pesticides leaves toxic gas residues in the home. See also **ASBESTOS, FORMALDEHYDE,** and **SICK–BUILDING SYNDROME.** (10, 15, 20, 32)

INDUSTRIAL POLLUTION. Particles (especially of metal dusts) and waste gases (especially carbon monoxide, sulfur oxides, and nitrogen oxides) that are waste products of industry and end up in the air. Industrial emissions are the second largest polluters of the atmosphere after automotive exhausts.

The major industrial polluters include petroleum refining, metal smelting, iron foundries, the paper industry, coal cleaning and refuse operations, coke production for steel manufacture, iron and steel mills, grain mills and the flour handling industry, cement manufacture, and the phosphate fertilizer industry. The most common factory air pollutant of a chemical nature is methylene chloride.

Industrial pollution is a major cause of smog in urban areas. It may cause acute health problems in workers who receive heavy exposures to pollutants. And it may aggravate the respiratory and other health problems of people who live near the factories. (7, 25, 26, 35)

INFRARED RADIATION. Heat, or thermal, radiation received from the sun. Its frequency or wavelength is longer than that of visible light. It is the energy source for the reactions that create photochemical smog. Atmospheric pollutants, including dust, block the quantities of radiation received or reflected by the earth. Carbon dioxide especially plays a major role in preventing the reflection of infrared radiation back into space. This action may contribute to global warming. See also **GLOBAL WARMING, GREENHOUSE EFFECT,** and **PHOTOCHEMICAL AIR POLLUTION.**

INORGANIC POLLUTANTS. Chemical substances in the atmosphere, including many types of nitrates, sulfates, chlorides, and oxides. Tiny particles of these chemicals may combine with atmospheric water vapor and contribute to acid rain and its damaging effects.

Metals are the other major class of inorganic pollutants found in the air, usually as a result of industry. These include minute particles of antimony, beryllium, bismuth, cadmium, cobalt, copper, chromium, iron, lead, manganese, molybdenum, nickel, silver, tin, titanium, vanadium, and zinc. They may be present either in their pure states or in compounds, especially oxides. Many of the metals are toxic to plants, animals, and humans.

INSECTICIDES. Chemicals that kill insects. Insecticides are usually sprayed from the air. Most of the spray settles on the ground, where it may contaminate water, soil, and dust. But some aerosols remain airborne and can be spread by the wind.

A powder of white crystals, lindane ($C_6II_6Cl_6$) is one of the most widely used insecticides, particularly for ants and termites. It has a musty odor. The substance is a suspected carcinogen. Lindane has been found in soils and airborne dusts as well as in water and food supplies.

Chlordane is another powerful insecticide. Related to DDT, chlordane has been banned in several states and may only be used by professional exterminators. Weight loss, convulsions, and damage to kidneys and liver are among the symptoms of chlordane exposure.

A number of the insecticides designed for use against ants and termites are suspected carcinogens. Many insecticides contain chemicals that are fat soluble. They can, therefore, build up in human fatty tissue. Some research indicates that the hydrocarbons in many insecticides may increase the risks of developing coronary heart disease and various cancers.

INTERNAL COMBUSTION ENGINE. A device that produces power by burning fuels in a series of controlled explosions that take place inside the engine. A mixture of air and fuel is fed into a small chamber where the combustion takes place. This drives a piston that converts the chemical energy of the combustion process into mechanical energy. Automobiles, trucks, and other vehicles use the internal combustion engine for power.

Internal combustion engines are the greatest single source of atmospheric pollutants. These include the products of fuel combustion: carbon monoxide, oxides of nitrogen and sulfur, soot, and other hydrocarbons. They may also emit particles of lead. But lead emissions have been reduced by the introduction of lead-free gasoline and use of the catalytic converter. Small quantities of heavy metal particles that occur as contaminants in gasoline, kerosene, and diesel fuels continue to contaminate the air. See also **AUTOMOBILE EXHAUST.**

IONOSPHERE. See **ATMOSPHERE.**

ISOPRENE (C_5H_8). A colorless hydrocarbon liquid that is a basic component of natural and synthetic rubbers. Sunlight causes the trees in rainforests to release isoprene into the air. The more sunlight there is, the more isoprene is released. Isoprene is an example of a naturally produced substance that can have a significant impact on overall atmospheric pollution. Isoprene is also released in automobile exhaust.

Isoprene reacts with the molecules formed when sunlight breaks down ozone. This produces carbon monoxide, which combines with oxygen to form carbon dioxide. This process tends to increase atmospheric levels of carbon dioxide, one of the gases that contributes to global warming. See also **GLOBAL WARMING** and **GREEN-HOUSE EFFECT.**

K

KILLER (LONDON) FOGS. Severe pollution incidents that occurred when the air became overloaded with pollutants from smoke. A number of these killer fogs took place in the city of London, England, during the winter months and often lasted for weeks at a time. The main health hazard was from the droplets of sulfuric acid that people breathed into their lungs. The acid was formed from the sulfur dioxide released by the burning of soft coal.

In 1952 the most famous of the London "killer" fogs claimed some 4,000 lives within two weeks. All of these deaths were due to respiratory failure. The atmosphere became so thick that the brownish haze seeped into houses around doors and windows and even through keyholes. In the two months following, another 8,000 people died from lung damage caused by the fogs.

In 1972, in one of the last of London's killer fogs, some 750 people died. Because of the changeover in recent years to fuel oil and natural gas for heating and industry, killer fogs seem to have disappeared.

L

LASER BEAMS. Narrow, intense beams of concentrated light of a single wavelength. The acronym *lasers* comes from *L*ight *A*mplification by *S*timulated *E*mmission of *R*adiation. Laser beams have been proposed as a solution to at least part of the problem of atmospheric contamination. If mounted at the industrial sources of harmful chemicals, lasers could blast apart molecules of the substances before they have a chance to enter the atmosphere. Scientists estimate that a million tons of ozone-destroying CFCs a year—equal to the current world output—could be rendered harmless by this method.

LEAD (Pb). A heavy metal that is highly toxic and is a common atmospheric pollutant. Everyone has some lead in his or her body. It is one of the most dangerous by-products of car exhaust. In today's cities, children exposed to traffic fumes have higher than average amounts of lead in their blood. Dust containing high levels of lead and other toxins is frequently found in incinerator wastes. Lead particles are commonly found in soil and dust because there is so much lead in the environment from sources ranging from water pipes to paints.

Lead is an additive used in gasoline to improve performance. In 1975 the U.S. Congress passed a law requiring the use of lead-free gasoline. After car engines had been changed so that most cars could run on lead-free gas, the amount of lead in the blood of the average American dropped as much as 38 percent.

Just a small amount of lead can cause developmental problems in children. Pregnant women exposed to lead may give birth to children with mental and physical problems. More severe lead poisoning may cause seizures. Lead interferes with enzyme actions in the body. It is absorbed into the bones, and if blood levels drop, the bones may release more lead into the bloodstream.

Low levels of lead in the body can cause digestive problems, hearing loss, and stunted growth. In middle-aged people lead poisoning can cause heart disease. Lead is toxic to humans because when it enters the bloodstream it causes red blood cells to rupture. It can also damage the brain, nervous system, and digestive tract. See also **AUTOMOBILE EXHAUST.**

LEGIONNAIRE'S DISEASE. A form of bacterial pneumonia that causes breathing problems and flulike symptoms. The disease was first encountered in 1976 and so named because it affected a group of people attending an American Legion convention at a hotel in Philadelphia. The bacteria that caused the disease were spread by the hotel's air conditioning and ventilating system. In this first recorded outbreak of the disease, 15 percent of those who became sick died as a result of it. From time to time new outbreaks of the disease have been linked to bacteria in ventilation equipment. Legionnaire's Disease is an example of the problems caused by bacterial pollution. See also **AIR CONDITIONERS, BACTERIAL POLLUTION,** and **INDOOR AIR POLLUTION.** (15)

LUNG CANCER. The growth of malignant tumors in the lungs. Lung cancer eventually destroys the lungs. Like other cancers, it can spread to other body parts. Lung cancer is the most common cancer killer of men in the 35–54 age group. There is clear evidence that exposure to tobacco smoke, radon gas, and coal or asbestos particles can lead to lung cancer.

A number of other substances have been clearly linked to the development of lung cancer. Workers exposed to arsenic, vinyl chloride, and coke oven emissions are especially at risk. Indoor levels of radon account for 10,000 to 20,000 additional deaths from lung cancer each year. Death rates for those known to have been exposed to high levels of radon are highest for victims who also smoked. Studies have found that the vapors from solvents, automotive fuels, and other chemicals may promote lung cancer. See also **ASBESTOS, CANCER, RADON,** and **TOBACCO SMOKE.**

M

MERCURY (Hg; also known as **QUICKSILVER**). A liquid metallic element that occurs in soil, rocks, air, and water. Mercury compounds may also appear as contaminants in fossil fuels such as coal and crude oil. The mercury they contain is released into the air when they are burned. About sixty different mercury compounds are used in agricultural pesticides, which end up in the air and in dust. Mercury compounds are also used in air conditioner filters and in paints and brushes. Mercury vapors can be a hazard in laboratories, including school labs. The substance can collect in cracks in wall, floor, or laboratory table surfaces and emit dangerous vapors.

Mercury enters the bloodstream through inhalation of its vapors. It can also be absorbed through the skin. Inside the body, mercury can damage the brain and nervous system. Some scientists think that the mercury amalgam commonly used in dental fillings may also give off minute amounts of mercury vapor. Traditional fillings are about 50 percent mercury.

METHANE (CH_4; also called **MARSH GAS** or **METHYL HYDRIDE**). A colorless, odorless, gaseous hydrocarbon. It is highly combustible and can form explosive mixtures with air. Methane occurs in nature as the principal ingredient of natural gas. It is formed by the bacterial decomposition of plant and animal matter. When this decomposition occurs underwater, marsh gas is released. The gas in coal mines is chiefly methane. Methane is also present in industrial emissions and automobile exhausts.

Methane is released in quantity by the bacteria in rice paddies and as a product of the digestive processes in animals such as cows and horses. Because the number of domesticated animals is increasing, the amount of methane being generated by these sources is also increasing. Atmospheric methane levels have doubled in the past three decades. Methane in the atmosphere absorbs heat. It is thus one of the principal gases believed to be causing the greenhouse effect. See also **GREENHOUSE EFFECT.** (3, 16)

METHYL ISOCYANATE (C_2H_3NO; abbreviated **MIC**). A highly flammable gas that breaks down in the air. Methyl isocyanate is used in the manufacture of pesticides. In 1984 a leak of more than five tons of the gas from a chemical plant in Bhopal, India, caused the worst industrial chemical disaster in history. Brain damage, permanent blindness, liver and kidney damage, and sterility are among the serious health problems induced by exposure to methyl isocyanate. See also **DISASTERS, POLLUTION–RELATED.**

METHYLENE CHLORIDE (CH_2Cl_2). A colorless, volatile liquid widely used in paint strippers, insecticides, and many aerosol paint products. Recent studies showed methylene chloride to be the most common chemical pollutant. Due to its industrial uses, there are many opportunities for the chemical to enter the atmosphere. Products that list "chlorinated solvents" or "aromatic hydrocarbons" among their ingredients probably contain methylene chloride. Until recently the chemical had been used to take caffeine out of coffee.

Exposure to methylene chloride reduces the blood's ability to carry oxygen. Tests show that methylene chloride can cause cancer in animals. The chemical may lead to cancers in humans as well.

MIST. Liquid particles that range in size from smaller than 0.1 micron up to 100 microns in diameter. Some mists are formed when pesticides, paints, or chemicals are sprayed. In nature, mists are formed by the condensation of vapor (especially water vapor) in the atmosphere or by the action of sunlight on photochemical oxidants. As mists evaporate, smaller aerosols are formed that contain less water. They are more chemically concentrated and can therefore be more dangerous to human health if they are inhaled.

MOLDS. A class of simple organisms, they are plant forms that cannot grow by themselves. Molds range in size from 5 to 10 microns. Although we associate them with dampness, molds need only minimum moisture to begin to grow. They grow in food or on dust as well as in ventilating systems, humidifiers, and air cooling and heating equipment. They are especially prevalent wherever humidity is high.

Molds often grow in bathrooms and showers as well as in the wood used in home construction. They can also grow in carpeting and upholstered furniture. Molds grow in soil, which may be outdoors or, in the case of potted plants, indoors. Many people are allergic to mold spores, and inhalation causes irritation of the respiratory tract. (15)

MONITORING. See **POLLUTION DETECTION AND MONITORING.**

N

NAPHTHA. One of a class of colorless, volatile, liquid hydrocarbon mixtures. It is used as a solvent for fats, rubber, and in the making of varnish. Because it dissolves grease easily, naphtha is often used as a cleaning fluid in certain soaps and detergents. Because it is an ingredient in everyday products, naphtha fumes from varnishes or cleaning products may be found in the home or work environment. As with other hydrocarbons, naphtha may cause eye irritation or respiratory problems. Prolonged inhalation of its vapors may cause liver or kidney damage. Naphtha may be carcinogenic.

NAPHTHALENE ($C_{10}H_8$). A colorless, crystalline, solid aromatic hydrocarbon with a strong odor. It is insoluble in water, but soluble in ether, chloroform, and carbon disulfide. Naphthalene is obtained from coal tar. It is a by-product of coal as it is made into coke. Because of its use in mothballs, naphthalene is a common indoor air pollutant. It is also used as an insect fumigant. Naphthalene is an irritant and is mildly toxic after prolonged inhalation.

NICKEL (Ni). A silvery, metallic, crystalline element. Nickel particles enter the atmosphere during industrial operations and in fly ash. In nature, nickel gets into the atmosphere when ore-containing rock weathers into dust.

Those exposed to nickel oxide dust have been found to have nickel absorbed into their hair. Hair samples can be used to determine the degree of nickel poisoning. Studies have shown that nickel causes dermatitis as well as cancers of the nasal passages, sinuses, and lungs.

NICOTINE. See **TOBACCO SMOKE.**

NITRIC OXIDE (NO). A colorless gas produced by high-temperature, high-pressure combustion. Thus its common source is from industrial processes. It is relatively unstable and oxidizes readily into nitrogen dioxide (NO_2). By binding with ozone's third oxygen atom, nitric oxide contributes to the destruction of ozone in the atmosphere.

NITROGEN DIOXIDE (NO_2). A gas that ranges in color from brown to orange, depending upon its concentration. Nitrogen dioxide is one of the major pollutants in automobile exhaust. The substance is also formed when foods burn and cause smoke. As a major component of photochemical smog it is an eye, mucous membrane, and respiratory tract irritant. See also **PHOTOCHEMICAL AIR POLLUTION.**

NITROGEN OXIDES. A group of chemical compounds made up of nitrogen and oxygen atoms. They are common air pollutants both indoors and outdoors.

The oxides of nitrogen have many properties in common. They are produced when natural gas or oil is burned in air that is rich in oxygen. Some oxides are formed when fuels are burned at high temperatures and then are permitted to cool quickly. Typical sources of nitrogen oxide and nitrogen dioxide include kitchen stoves and ovens, furnaces, kerosene heaters, and automobile engines. Nitrogen oxides are also produced by factories that manufacture fertilizer and explosives. Nitrogen oxides are a component of cigarette smoke and also occur in nature when leaves are burned. To prevent this, many communities now prohibit the burning of leaves in the autumn.

Scientists have recently discovered that the action of lightning on nitrogen gas in the air causes the formation of nitrogen oxides. Half of the nitrogen oxides found in the atmosphere come from lightning.

In small amounts nitrogen oxides can cause respiratory infections, but in larger doses they can cause death. Animal researchers have found a link between nitrogen oxides and emphysema. Infants and young children who are exposed to nitrogen oxides often develop respiratory infections.

NUCLEAR FALLOUT. The dust and debris from nuclear weapons that explode in the atmosphere. A nuclear explosion releases energy in the form of radioactive particles. These particles can injure and destroy plant and animal tissue. The heavier particles of fallout settle near the explosion site or somewhat downwind from it. Some particles are carried by winds throughout the earth's atmosphere. The lighter ones may remain suspended for years. Precipitation washes radioactive particles out of the atmosphere. They can then enter the food chain as they contaminate water supplies, pastures, and croplands. They are then taken up by plants and animals.

Particles of radioactive fallout can collect inside the human body. There the radioactive particles can cause radiation sickness, leukemia, and bone cancer as well as other cancers and diseases. Fallout has also been linked to chromosome damage, miscarriage, and birth defects. Most of the world's nations that have nuclear weapons no longer test them in the atmosphere. Therefore current levels of nuclear fallout are low. See also **NUCLEAR WINTER.** (4)

NUCLEAR POWER. The energy generated by radioactive fuels at nuclear plants. Nuclear power is often described as "clean" when compared with fossil fuels. Nuclear power may be one way to help limit air pollution problems, since nuclear power plants do not produce carbon dioxide or any of the gases that cause acid rain.

However, nuclear power facilities may present some danger. Radioactive products may escape from them and expose people in the vicinity to radioactive contamination. The proposed use of small nuclear explosions for building tunnels, dams, and harbors has been limited because of the danger.

Nuclear waste may emit dangerous gamma rays or nuclear particles that can damage human tissues and lead to tumor growth. See also **RADON.** (4)

NUCLEAR WINTER. A period of severe cold and wintry conditions that scientists predict would be the result of widespread nuclear war. The explosion of a number of nuclear weapons around the world would raise clouds of fine dust and debris. This dust would clog the stratosphere, blocking out sunlight. Winds in the upper atmosphere would carry the radioactive clouds over the whole earth. This condition would plunge the planet into a cold, dark period lasting months or even years, and all but the simplest forms of life would die.

O

ORGANIC VAPORS. Gases and particles formed from chemical compounds that contain the element carbon. Organic chemicals make up more than 98 percent of all chemical compounds.

Organic vapors are common air pollutants that enter the atmosphere by a number of natural and manmade processes. Evaporating fumes from alcohols, ethers, paints, lacquers, and thinners continuously contaminate the air. Many of these vapors have noticeable odors.

Hydrocarbons, fluorocarbons, and aromatics (a subclass of hydrocarbons made up of more than one ring) produce organic vapors. The class of hydrocarbons called terpenes (released by pine trees) creates the blue haze observable over forests. Automotive exhausts, industrial processes, the burning of fuels, and the decomposition of organisms on land and in the sea all release organic gases. Oil refineries and facilities store liquid fuels and other volatile liquids that may leak into the atmosphere.

OXYGEN (O_2). A colorless, odorless, and tasteless gas. Oxygen is a chemical element that is extremely active. It readily mixes with other elements to form compounds. Oxygen is the most abundant element and makes up about half the total mass of material of earth. Only a small proportion of the earth's total oxygen is found in air, which is only about one-fifth oxygen. Most of the world's oxygen is combined to form water, silicates, and other compounds such as oxides. Oxides of many different elements are among the principal air pollutants.

In many cases, an increase in the level of pollutants in the air means a decrease in the amount of oxygen available for breathing. This is especially true indoors or in any confined spaces where the other gases may displace all or most of the available oxygen. Carbon monoxide or freon, for example, may cause asphyxiation in this way.

OZONE (O_3). The ozone molecule consists of three atoms of oxygen loosely bonded together. It has a strong, pungent odor, and it reacts with many materials, including plant and animal tissues. Ozone is a component of smog formed by the interaction of sunlight and organic compounds from automobile exhaust and industrial processes.

Ozone is also a natural component of the atmosphere. Much of the ozone in the air is formed by the action of lightning bolts. However, in nature it occurs at low concentrations. Photochemical action in the atmosphere (smog) can raise ozone levels to ten times normal level.

In the earth's upper atmosphere, the ozone layer helps to shield the earth from the sun's ultraviolet radiation. Near the ground, ozone concentrations are normally low, but high levels have been found in air from rural mountain tops as well as in urban smog. Outdoors, ozone at ground level is hazardous to plants and animals. Sometimes ozone may be found indoors near electrostatic copying machines and air cleaners.

Ozone irritates the lungs, mucous membranes, and respiratory tissues. It also leads to the breakdown of products containing rubber.

OZONE HOLE. A gap in the layer of ozone that forms part of the stratosphere. Scientists have discovered that the layer of ozone that surrounds the earth appears to be thinning. Over the Poles, where the layer is thinnest, the problem seems to be worst. Chlorine gas appears to be responsible for this depletion of ozone. At first scientists thought that the chlorine might come from natural sources such as volcanic eruptions. But when fluorine gas molecules were found as well, scientists began to suspect the probable cause. Chlorofluorocarbon (CFC) propellants used in some spray cans appear to be doing the damage.

Scientists believe that molecules of CFCs drift up into the stratosphere where they release chlorine gas. The chlorine breaks ozone molecules apart. The ozone hole was first announced in 1985 by a British research team. Each September, as spring begins in the Southern Hemisphere, the atmosphere warms up. The chlorine gas then reacts more readily with ozone molecules. The amount of ozone in the ozone layer over the South Pole drops by as much as 50 percent.

Because the ozone layer absorbs ultraviolet radiation from the sun, depletion of the ozone layer means that higher levels of radiation reach the earth's surface. Scientists believe the incidence of skin cancers and cataracts will rise sharply. Satellite measurements taken between 1979 and 1986 showed an overall drop of about 5 percent in ozone levels. In the United States alone, this could mean up to 40,000 new cases of skin cancer per year.

OZONE LAYER. Part of the atmosphere about 12 to 30 miles (20 to 48 kilometers) above the earth. This layer shields the earth's surface and the plants and animals that live there from dangerous levels of ultraviolet radiation from the sun. Ozone molecules absorb most of this radiation. Still, enough radiation filters through to cause many people to develop skin cancers and cataracts. There is evidence that pollutants are damaging the ozone layer. See also **OZONE HOLE.**

P

PARADICHLOROBENZENE ($C_6H_4Cl_2$). A volatile, white, crystalline chemical made by chlorinating benzene. In its solid form it is used to make mothballs that protect furs and woolens from insect damage. Most mothballs are pure paradichlorobenzene, and their toxic vapors are a common source of indoor air pollution.

Paradichlorobenzene is a known irritant of skin and eyes. Short-term exposure irritates the nasal passages, throat, and lungs and causes depression. Long-term exposure can lead to liver and kidney damage.

PARAQUAT ($C_{12}H_{14}N_2$). A white, crystalline substance. A potent herbicide, designed to kill weeds, paraquat has been used on millions of acres of United States farmland. The U.S. government has used the substance to kill marijuana crops. Paraquat aerosols can be carried by the wind when fields are being sprayed. Humans and animals exposed to paraquat may develop respiratory or other diseases. Even small doses can cause death if they are swallowed or inhaled. Marijuana users may be exposed to the poison when they smoke.

PARTICULATE MATTER. Tiny pieces, or particles, of both natural and manmade solid matter found in the atmosphere. These pieces consist of fine dust, coarse dust, fumes, and mists. Most airborne particles are found in the layer of atmosphere within two miles of earth. Particulate pollutants are dispersed as airborne liquid or solid particles larger than single molecules but smaller than 500 microns. Fine dust is less than 100 microns in diameter. Coarse dust, or grit, is greater than 100 microns. Fumes contain the smallest particles, from 0.001 to 1 micron. And mist ranges from 0.01 to 10 microns in diameter. Particles stay in the air from a few seconds to several months or years. Larger particles, including pieces of ash from coal fires, may stay in the air only briefly. Many of these particles serve as condensation nuclei.

Rain and snow clear particulate matter from the atmosphere. Drizzle and wet fog are the most efficient air cleaners. Most of the time gravity makes the particles settle as dust. This settling occurs more readily when the air is still.

Most particulate matter in the atmosphere comes from natural sources. Sea salt, soil dust, pollen grains, bacteria, and volcanic dust and ash are all common natural particulates.

Manmade particles are usually smaller in size, stay in the air longer, and are more damaging to human health and the environment. Minute metal particles enter the atmosphere in fly ash. Worldwide, industry adds about 200,000,000 tons of manmade particulates to the atmosphere each year. These pollutants include dust, soot, and ashes from combustion and incineration. The burning of fossil fuels adds more than a half billion tons of matter to the atmosphere each year. Automobile exhaust spews many particulates, including toxic lead particles, into the air. Every time an airplane lands or takes off, it pumps approximately 140 pounds (63.4 kilograms) of particulate matter into the atmosphere.

Health statistics show that levels of particulate matter above 100 micrograms per cubic meter of air increase the death rates for persons over fifty and increase the likelihood of childhood respiratory diseases. Yet many cities have average daily concentrations twice or occasionally as much as five times this recognized danger level. See also **CONDENSATION NUCLEI** and **DUST**.

PERCHLOROETHYLENE (CCl_2CCl_2; also known as **CARBON DICHLORIDE** or **TETRACHLOROETHYLENE**). A colorless liquid, with an odor like chloroform. Perchloroethylene is the solvent most commonly used by commercial dry cleaners and in over-the-counter spot removers. It is a skin and eye irritant. The chemical is toxic when inhaled. Studies show that its fumes can cause lightheadedness, drowsiness, vertigo, appetite loss, confusion, and depression of the central nervous system. Perchloroethylene has been linked to liver damage and various cancers.

PEROXYACETYL NITRATE ($CH_3COOONO_2$; abbreviated **PAN**; also known as **ACETYL NITROPEROXIDE**). An organic gas, PAN is a secondary pollutant produced by photochemical action. Solar energy acts on nitric oxide and hydrocarbons from automobile exhausts to form PAN. High levels of PAN in smog cause stinging and eye irritation and aggravate respiratory problems. It also causes damage to plants.

PHENOL (C_6H_5OH). One of a class of related organic liquids that are generally colorless. Phenols are common air contaminants in industrial emissions. Chlorinated phenols—used in many herbicides, pesticides, and wood preservatives—are even more hazardous. The breakdown of chlorinated phenols produces dioxins, among the most toxic of all wastes.

Phenols are powerful irritants of skin, mucous membranes, and respiratory passages. Exposure over time leads to organ damage and various cancers.

PHOSGENE ($COCl_2$; also known as **CARBON OXYCHLORIDE** or **CARBONYL CHLORIDE**). A colorless gas or liquid that is highly toxic. Phosgene smells much like freshly cut grass. At high temperatures carbon tetrachloride may form phosgene. Chloroform can also break down in sunlight to form phosgene. When inhaled, it reacts with moisture in the lungs to make hydrochloric acid and carbon monoxide. Phosgene is a very powerful eye, throat, and lung irritant.

PHOTOCHEMICAL AIR POLLUTION (Also called **SECONDARY POLLUTION**). Pollution that forms in the atmosphere when sunlight acts on gases that come mainly from automobile exhausts. A well-known example of the formation of photochemical, or secondary, pollutants is the smog for which Los Angeles has become famous. Hydrocarbons and nitric oxide from exhaust are turned into ozone, nitrogen dioxide, and peroxyacetyl nitrate (PAN).

Smog often occurs in nonindustrial cities with warm, dry climates. The source of most of this smog is car exhaust, in the form of nitric oxide. This combines with oxygen in the atmosphere to form nitrogen dioxide, a reddish brown gas that gives smog its color. The smog can irritate eyes, corrode building materials, injure plants, and cause some fabrics to decay. It can also cause headaches, bronchitis, and lung diseases. See also **PEROXYACETYL NITRATE, SECONDARY POLLUTANTS,** and **SMOG.**

POLLEN. Tiny particles of organic matter, often yellow, produced by flowering plants. Pollen grains range in size from 15 to 35 microns. They contain material necessary for plant reproduction.

Pollen is a major component of dust, particularly during spring, summer, and autumn. The wind carries millions of pollen grains from place to place. In this way they contaminate clean air. Pollen grains may irritate nose and throat passages and cause allergic reactions. Goldenrod and ragweed produce great amounts of pollen, which causes hay fever. Hay fever is not really a fever but an allergic reaction that causes watery eyes and blocks breathing passages.

POLLUTION CONCENTRATION, DETERMINANTS OF. Measurements of air pollutants are usually expressed as parts per million (ppm) parts of air. Sometimes measurements are stated in terms of the total weight of particles or of the quantity of a specific gas within a standard volume of air. The usual measurement is a cubic meter. Where an air sample is taken will affect the reading. The distance from the pollution source and whether the reading is taken upwind or downwind from the source also make a difference. The measurement may record the level at a single instant. Or, it may be a continuous reading of levels recorded over a twenty-four-hour period. Whether the wind has dispersed the pollutants or whether the air is still, as during a temperature inversion, are also factors that influence the level of air pollution. Precipitation, especially mist and fog, may wash many pollutants out of the air. A steady rain or snow can have the same cleaning effect.

In general, people breathing polluted air may experience discomfort, but may not be certain why. It is difficult to know what is in the air one is breathing. Even scientists do not know without first performing tests. The general public, therefore, must rely on meteorological readings and pollution level reports.

POLLUTION CONTROL DEVICES. Devices to remove waste substances from the air during industrial processes. Filters, scrubbers, and electrostatic precipitators are used to help clean the air from factories and power plants by trapping some of the emissions before they leave the smokestacks.

Particulate emissions are the easiest air pollutants to control. Tubular filters, made from durable cloth or various synthetic fibers, can remove particles of various sizes. Gravity settlers are collecting chambers in which large particles can settle out of a stream of waste gases. Wet scrubbers are devices that rely upon liquid or foam spray to intercept particles or gases.

Gaseous contaminants are somewhat difficult to control. Limiting the amounts of these pollutants in the air often involves a combination of physical and chemical techniques, including carbon filters and wet scrubbing devices. Activated charcoal filters can be used to remove hydrocarbon gases. But large amounts of contaminants may still be released into the atmosphere.

Sulfur dioxide can be removed by passing the air through activated charcoal filters. Sometimes air containing sulfur dioxide is bubbled through an alkaline solution or sprayed. The gas is thus turned into sulfuric acid, which is then removed. See also **ACTIVATED CARBON, BAGHOUSE,** and **SCRUBBERS.** (7, 22, 25, 33, 34)

POLLUTION DETECTION AND MONITORING. Finding, identifying, measuring, and recording the levels of gaseous and particulate pollutants in the air. Permanent laboratories located at airports, on roofs of buildings, and at weather stations continuously collect data. Mobile laboratory units collect samples and measure the air quality at factory and incineration sites. Computers record and interpret this information. Public health warnings are issued if air pollution exceeds established limits.

In 1953 the National Air Sampling Network was established. It consists of hundreds of recording stations located across the country. Every fourteen days each station in the network monitors the levels of dust, fly ash, soot, and other matter collected during a twenty-four-hour period. The samples are examined, analyzed, and compared with readings from other stations in the network.

A dustfall collector is one of the most basic tools. It collects particles large enough to settle out by gravity. These include various kinds of dust, soot, ash, metal particles, and plant material such as pollen grains or spores. The contents are weighed and analyzed.

Special filters collect air samples for analysis by researchers. Microscopic examination can reveal biological pollutants—bacteria, molds, and fungi or plant debris.

Most air sampling takes place near the ground. Sometimes airborne laboratories mounted on helicopters, dirigibles, or other aircraft use vacuum pumps to collect air samples from different altitudes. Such mobility makes it easier to get very near pollution sources—for example, in the air near manufacturing plants and industrial smokestacks.

Ultraviolet photometry or chemoluminescence determine the chemical nature of the pollutants. Delicate instruments measure the ways different gases in the atmosphere refract or bend light.

Air pollution emergencies are declared when levels of pollutants exceed a predetermined amount. Special precautionary steps are taken to minimize the pollution, which may include banning open fires, shutting down incinerators, or reducing industrial operations. (19, 22, 29, 33, 34)

POLLUTION, EFFECTS ON LIVING THINGS. Air pollution reduces agricultural productivity. It also causes forests around the world to decline. Emissions from power plants, factories, and motor vehicles are all increasing atmospheric levels of ozone, acid-forming air pollutants, and carbon dioxide, as well as the other greenhouse gases.

Pollution decreases the amount of sunlight that can reach plants. It can also coat leaves and needles and block plant respiration. Plant and tree damage is first noted at higher elevations and then spreads to lower level sites among a wider variety of plant species. This pattern has been noted in Central Europe, where pollution-related problems have plagued forests for decades.

Tree damage has been reported in many parts of the United States and around the world. Pine trees in California, sugar maples in the Northeast, and spruce and fir trees in the Appalachians have all been affected. The decline in growth rates of Southeast yellow pines has also been traced to high ozone concentrations.

Crop damage accounts for lost revenues from crops as diverse as soy beans, peanuts, wheat, and coffee. In the United States, farmers lose billions of dollars each year due to pollution.

Environmental pollution has also led to biological adaptations.

Since the Industrial Revolution, generations of peppered moths have mutated to display darker coloration. This change in their protective coloration mimics the patterns of soot on the bark of the trees where they live. It has helped them to escape the notice of the birds that feed on them. Now that much smoke has been controlled, the moths have shed some of their coloration. They can thus blend in more readily in the lighter, cleaner background.

The future may show other effects of pollution on living things. Scientists feel that the increase in greenhouse gases may benefit some plants. Most plants show somewhat faster growth rates in the higher carbon dioxide levels, and many plants actually thrive in the new, warmer temperatures observed in some areas.

POLYCHLORINATED BIPHENYLS (PCBs). Highly toxic liquids similar to the chlorinated phenols used in the manufacture of herbicides and pesticides. PCBs were once used in electrical transformers. They are still used in making duplicating papers and certain types of plastics. Millions of pounds are released by businesses annually, usually in liquid form, even though PCBs have been banned for most uses since the late 1970s.

PCBs are not readily biodegradable and resist breakdown by heat, light, water, acids, and alkalis. In the environment, PCBs occur mainly in an oil solution. Industrial fires often burn waste oils contaminated with PCBs. This creates toxic smoke containing vaporized PCBs and PCB by-products. Partially burned PCBs can release even more deadly atmospheric pollutants: furans and dioxins. Incinerators that operate at too low a temperature prompt the formation of these dangerous by-products.

Studies have linked environmental PCBs to brain, nerve, liver, and skin disorders. The chemicals have also produced malignant tumors in rats.

POLYSTYRENE ($C_6H_5CH-CH_2$).   A widely-used, colorless, transparent plastic. Polystyrene can be a solid or a foam plastic, known as styrofoam. The material is used in insulation and packaging materials. Polystyrene enters the atmosphere during manufacturing operations and when the tiny bubbles in plastic foam rupture. The chemical is believed to be carcinogenic.

POLYURETHANES. A group of plastics that can be made into both rigid and flexible foams. In its flexible form it is used for seat cushions, mattresses, and carpet backing. In its rigid form it is often used in insulation, furniture, and building materials. Aerosols of polyurethane may enter the atmosphere during many manufacturing operations. Combustion of materials containing polyurethane releases toxic gases, including dioxins and hydrocarbons. In addition to irritating breathing passages, the vapors may be carcinogenic.

POWER PLANT EMISSIONS. The smoke and waste gases from plants that produce electrical power. Fossil fuels such as coal and oil that are burned to generate power contain much sulfur. Power plants are the largest producers of sulfur oxide emissions, particularly sulfur dioxide. Power plants are the third largest single source of atmospheric pollutants—after transportation exhausts and industrial process wastes. In general, nuclear power plants produce no emissions, except in cases of accidental radiation release. See also **FOSSIL FUELS** and **POLLUTION CONTROL DEVICES.**

PRIMARY POLLUTANTS. Contaminating substances that enter the atmosphere directly from pollution sources. Carbon monoxide, sulfur dioxide, and certain hydrocarbons are examples of primary pollutants. Primary pollutants and atmospheric gases and particles react in the presence of heat and light energy to form secondary pollutants in the atmosphere itself. See also **PHOTOCHEMICAL AIR POLLUTION.**

R

RADON (Rn). An invisible, colorless, odorless gas usually found in rock formations. Granite and other hard, igneous (fire-produced) or metamorphic (transformed) rocks that yield radium and uranium ores can produce high levels of radon. The breakdown of the radioactive elements radium and uranium produces radon gas. Radon occurs naturally in some spring waters, streams, and soils.

Radon is one of the primary indoor pollutants. The gas seeps slowly through air pockets in the ground. It enters homes and other buildings through cracks in the foundations or through other openings. In the winter, indoor levels of radon increase sharply since lack of ventilation tends to keep the gas inside. Heating systems act almost as pumps to draw radon out of the soil and into structures. There may be as many as eight million homes in the United States where radon levels are dangerously high. A rock formation called the Reading Prong that runs under portions of Pennsylvania, New York, and New Jersey has high concentrations of uranium. Surveys conducted indicate that 40 percent of the homes tested in this area had levels of radon exceeding EPA safety limits.

Radon is responsible for some 20,000 to 30,000 cancer deaths annually. The U.S. Public Health Service has estimated that between 10 and 20 percent of people who have worked as uranium miners will eventually die of lung cancer. This cancer was caused, at least in part, by inhalation of radon gas. Radon has also been linked to cancers of the bones, skin, and blood cells, although the effects may not be felt for ten to fifteen years. Especially at risk are people who live in areas where uranium or radium have been mined. (13, 18)

RAIN FORESTS. Areas of the world where heavy rainfall sustains a lush growth of vegetation—primarily trees. Although the largest tracts of rain forest are in South America, there are also extensive areas of Southeast Asia and Africa that are considered rain forests. Around the world, however, rain forests are disappearing at an alarming rate. The figures vary, but many sources say that between 24,000 and 30,000 square miles (62,000 and 80,000 square kilometers) of rain forest are disappearing every year.

Rain forests are important because they help to regulate atmospheric conditions. The fires caused by settlers clearing rain forest in South America contributed 10 percent of the global atmospheric carbon dioxide produced in 1987. At the same time that carbon dioxide levels increase as plants are burned, the level of oxygen decreases—since rain forest plants release oxygen during photosynthesis. The loss of trees means that fewer plants remain to use up atmospheric carbon dioxide in their respiration and photosynthesis.

Scientists think that excess carbon dioxide in the atmosphere absorbs more of the sun's heat, contributing to the so-called greenhouse effect. Because trees—especially mature, older ones—use so much carbon dioxide, tree maintenance and reforestation efforts are important factors in maintaining balance in the earth's atmosphere and climate. See also **GLOBAL WARMING** and **GREENHOUSE EFFECT.** (21)

REFRIGERANTS. Chemical compounds that absorb heat and lower the temperature of surrounding air as the refrigerant liquid changes to a gas. Mechanical refrigeration systems used in refrigerators, freezers, and air conditioners are all based on this principle. Freon (a CFC) and ammonia compounds are the most commonly used refrigerants today.

A pressurized system circulates the refrigerant through coils where the refrigerant vaporizes and liquifies, removing heat. However, refrigeration systems frequently spring leaks that allow some of the liquid refrigerant to escape. The refrigerant vaporizes readily and pollutes the air. In closed spaces CFC vapors can be toxic. In the atmosphere CFCs damage the ozone layer. See also **CHLORO-FLUOROCARBONS, OZONE HOLE, OZONE LAYER,** and **TRICHLOROTRIFLUOROETHANE.**

RESPIRABLE FIBERS. Any fibrous particles small enough to be inhaled. Dust and lint from the cotton industry and particles of crumbling asbestos are two of the most common and dangerous respirable fibers. Cotton dust is a fine powder resulting from the manufacture of cotton. Inhalation of cotton dust, coal dust, and asbestos fibers can all trigger asthma attacks as well as more serious respiratory diseases. Over a period of time, particles can lead to the formation of lung tumors. See also **ASBESTOS** and **BLACK/BROWN LUNG DISEASE.**

ROTTEN EGG GAS. See **HYDROGEN SULFIDE.**

S

SCRUBBERS. Pollution control devices used in industry to remove aerosols and waste gases. Wet scrubbers direct sprays of water or other liquids into a chamber containing exhaust gases. The contaminants are then washed away in the liquid. Other methods of removing gases include adsorption by activated charcoal and filtering.

SECONDARY POLLUTANTS. Pollutants that are not released into the air directly but are formed by natural processes acting on primary pollutants in the air. Most secondary pollutants are the result of photochemical reactions, as the sun's rays cause chemical changes to airborne pollutants. The ozone and peroxyacetyl nitrate (PAN) in smog are produced as secondary pollutants. See also **PEROXYACETYL NITRATE, PHOTOCHEMICAL AIR POLLUTION, PRIMARY POLLUTANTS,** and **SMOG.**

SICK–BUILDING SYNDROME. An extreme example of indoor air pollution. Sometimes a large number of people who live or work in the same building all experience similar symptoms of illness. These problems may include headaches, nausea, breathing difficulties, or skin rashes caused by some health hazard in the building itself. The people affected are said to be suffering from what is known as sick building syndrome. "Sick buildings" usually have high levels of ozone, carbon monoxide, and formaldehyde, or other pollutants.

Surveys have shown that half the occupants of sick buildings are victims of chronic headaches and eye irritation.

The syndrome is believed to account for millions of lost workdays each year. Twenty to thirty percent of the office workers in the United States and Europe suffer from sick building syndrome. Poor building maintenance and inadequate or contaminated ventilating systems contribute to the problem. Smoking is a major polluter of indoor air. Copying machines foul the air in offices with hydrocarbon particles from inks and solvents and ozone produced by machine operations.

Because pollutants are often present in small quantities, they are difficult to trace. They may also be invisible and odorless. Often the levels of individual pollutants are within acceptable guidelines, but when they act together their effects are intensified. See also **INDOOR AIR POLLUTION.**

SILICA (SiO_2; also called **SILICON DIOXIDE** or **SAND**). One of the most common substances in the environment. Silica is composed of colorless crystals. The natural causes of silica dust in the atmosphere are wind action on soil dusts and ocean churning. Industrial sources include the glass industry, in which sand is a major raw material. Silica dust is also a component of fly ash from the burning of fossil fuels.

Silicosis is the most common dust-related disease. It results from inhaling quartz dust or other silica-containing dust. Shortness of breath, decreased lung capacity, and increased susceptibility to tuberculosis and other lung diseases are other symptoms of silica-related diseases.

SKIN CANCER. A disease characterized by the abnormal growth of skin cells. It is one of the easiest cancers to treat. But if it is not cured in time, skin cancer can lead to cancers elsewhere in the body.

The National Academy of Sciences estimates that 80 percent of skin cancers are due to exposure to ultraviolet rays from the sun. The group also estimates that 40 percent of melanomas (cancerous growths of pigment cells) are caused by the same type of exposure. Skin cancers are most common on the face, hands, and neck—those body parts that are exposed the most. Fair-skinned people are at great risk, as are those living in sunny areas. In the South, the melanoma rate is 75 percent higher than in the North.

Each year in the United States there are some 300,000 new cases of skin cancer. This cancer is one of the most curable types. It causes only about 5,000 deaths annually.

The thinning of the ozone layer allows higher levels of ultraviolet radiation to reach the earth. Already scientists have noted an increase in the incidence of skin cancer. Younger and younger patients are developing skin tumors or showing premature aging of the skin. See also **CANCER** and **OZONE LAYER.**

SMOG. A combination of *sm*oke and f*og*. Smog is a mixture of gaseous and particulate pollutants. It is largely caused by the action of ultraviolet light energy on sulfur dioxide, nitric oxide, ozone, and exhaust gases. For this reason, it is often called photochemical smog. Smog occurs in large cities around the world where traffic and automobile exhaust problems are enormous.

One city with a continuing smog problem is Los Angeles, California. At the beginning of this century Los Angeles had more than 350 clear days. By the 1940s, fewer than 100 clear days were being recorded.

Smog is not just an American problem. In Mexico City (the world's largest city), school hours have been adjusted so that people can cope with the periods of densest smog during the day. Smog also occurs in many cities in the Soviet Union. The city of Leningrad has 40 percent fewer clear daylight hours than smaller towns located nearby.

Sometimes smog is severe enough to require a health alert advising the sick and elderly to remain inside. Smog is an eye and respiratory irritant and can aggravate many existing health problems including lung and cardiovascular diseases. See also **PHOTO-CHEMICAL AIR POLLUTION.**

SMOKE. A mixture of solid particles and gases suspended in air. Its composition and characteristics vary as much as its sources.

Coal smoke contains carbon particles suspended in hydrocarbon gases. Dark in color, it is a product of incomplete combustion. The refining of metal ores produces smoke containing metal particles. Zinc and tin smoke are particularly damaging to vegetation.

The smoke from wood stoves and fireplaces contains hydrocarbon particles and carbon monoxide gas. Airtight stoves that burn wood slowly release microscopic particles of incompletely burned wood. The EPA classifies these particles as carcinogenic. Some new wood stoves have catalytic combustion devices similar to those used in automobiles.

On calm days, when the air above is cooler than air near the ground, smoke rises and disperses. If it is windy, however, smoke may be blown back toward the ground. In the city of Denver, Colorado, wood smoke and automobile exhaust create serious air pollution problems during winter periods when there is little wind.

SMOKING. See **TOBACCO SMOKE.**

SOLVENT FUMES. Solvents are organic chemicals that can dissolve materials that are not soluble in water. They are usually volatile liquids that are released into the atmosphere during industrial processes.

The release of solvent fumes can often be controlled through the use of afterburning devices. These are special chimney fittings that collect and combust waste gases before they are vented to the outside. Other processes use activated carbon filters that adsorb the fumes.

Among the best solvents are acetone, alcohol, benzene, carbon disulfide, carbon tetrachloride, chloroform, ether, ethyl acetate, furfural (a furan), gasoline, toluene, turpentine, and xylene. Most of these substances are toxic. Many of them have been linked to cancers and other health problems. Carbon tetrachloride, for example, is toxic in confined spaces and can produce phosgene. Toluene and xylene, both hydrocarbon solvents, are flammable, and their fumes can damage varnished surfaces.

SOOT (Also called **CARBON BLACK, BONE BLACK,** or **LAMP BLACK**). Particles of partially combusted matter in smoke. Soot is mostly carbon and is dark brown to black in color. It consists of very fine carbon particles clustered together in long, loose chains. Because the particles are so fine, they present an extremely large surface area. Carbon molecules are chemically active. Therefore soot particles tend to attract and adsorb a variety of chemicals from the surrounding air.

A common air contaminant, soot is a known irritant and a carcinogen. Tiny particles of soot may carry carcinogenic hydrocarbon molecules or other chemical impurities in the air deep into the lungs and breathing passages. There the particles may cause disease. Soot also dirties clothing and buildings.

SPACE, POLLUTION IN. Scientists are already becoming concerned about a growing pollution problem in space, just beyond the earth's atmosphere. Debris from spent rockets, satellites that no longer function, and other junk spinning in space could cause accidents as they collide with spacecraft. These objects range in size from dust particles to large chunks of metal. They could interfere with the earth's reception of solar radiation. Plans call for "space vacuums" that will collect the flying garbage. Large chunks of some spacecraft may fall out of orbit and come crashing back to earth. When NASA builds its space station the structure will need to have double walls to protect it from space debris.

STACK GASES (or **FLUE GASES**). Contaminants emitted by smokestacks. Consisting largely of oxides of sulfur and nitrogen, stack gases result from combustion and other industrial processes. See also **INDUSTRIAL POLLUTION.**

STRATOSPHERE. See **ATMOSPHERE.**

STRONTIUM (Sr). A chemical element that is a silver-yellow metal. Strontium is a component of nuclear fallout. Radioactive particles of the element entered the atmosphere and environment in the 1940s and 1950s when a number of nuclear weapons were tested aboveground. Since then, most nations no longer allow testing in the atmosphere.

Because it resembles calcium, strontium may find its way into milk and other foods. Therefore, strontium may be absorbed in the bones instead of calcium. In this way the substance may cause bone cancer and leukemia in young children. See also **NUCLEAR FALLOUT.**

SULFATES. A group of compounds containing the sulfate group, SO_4. Many industrial processes release sulfates into the atmosphere. They are found in automobile exhaust and are one of the components of particulate matter in the atmosphere. Sulfuric acid is the most common sulfate. It forms when sulfur dioxide or sulfur trioxide in the air combines with water.

SULFUR DIOXIDE (SO_2). A colorless gas with an intense odor. The gas tends to produce a tight, choking feeling in the throat. The chemical compound is highly soluble in water and thus forms sulfurous acid (H_2SO_3). Sulfur dioxide is produced by the combustion of coal, fuel oil, and gasoline. Sulfur dioxide is used in bleaching, as a refrigerant, and as a spray for certain fruits.

Sulfur dioxide emissions are a principal cause of acid rain. The sulfur content can be reduced by chemically refining the fuel. Less sulfur dioxide is then emitted when the fuel is burned.

In the air the inhalation of sulfur dioxide fumes causes damage to the lungs and respiratory system. Sulfur dioxide is irritating to the nose and throat in concentrations as low as 6 to 12 ppm. Even concentrations of less than 1 ppm may be tasted or smelled.

SULFUR OXIDES. A family of gases, the most common of which is sulfur dioxide. Sulfur oxides enter the atmosphere through industrial emissions and fuel combustion, especially by electric power plants. The power industry is the largest producer of sulfur oxides. Sulfur oxides are harmful to plants and people and corrosive to building materials. (30)

SULFUR TRIOXIDE (SO_3). A colorless crystal, gas, or liquid. The chemical is soluble in water vapor to form sulfuric acid (H_2SO_4), which is highly corrosive. Sulfuric acid is a component of acid rain. Most sulfur trioxide begins as sulfur dioxide from the combustion of fuels. The sulfur dioxide is slowly oxidized to become sulfur trioxide. The corrosive substance is known to destroy animal tissues.

SULFURIC ACID (H_2SO_4). A colorless, odorless, oily liquid. It is one of the most widely used industrial chemicals, and its mist escapes into the atmosphere. It is therefore a major air pollutant. More sulfuric acid is used annually than any other industrial chemical. It is used to produce fertilizers, wash impurities out of gasoline and other petroleum products, clean and process metals, make rayon, and manufacture lead-acid storage batteries for automobiles.

Sulfuric acid attacks the lungs and synthetic fabrics and eats away stone and metal in buildings. An exposure of 10 to 20 ppm causes severe chemical burns. Lesser exposures can cause irritation of eyes, mucous membranes, and the respiratory tract and cases of bronchitis.

T

TAILINGS. Tailings are the waste material from the processing of uranium ores. They are one source of radioactive radon gas and of toxic heavy metals that enter the air when wind makes the minute crushed ore particles airborne. The highest concentrations of these radioactive particles are found in the air near waste storage sites. But winds can spread radioactive dust over large areas hundreds of miles from the original source. (4)

TEMPERATURE INVERSION (or THERMAL INVERSION). An atmospheric condition in which a warm, high layer of air prevents air heated at ground level from rising. Air temperatures are normally cooler at higher altitudes. In a temperature inversion, warm air at high altitudes forms a blanket over cooler air below. Even when the cooler air heats up it cannot rise. This keeps the air at ground level from moving and carrying away the smoke, dust, or pollutants in it.

TERPENES ($C_{10}H_{16}$). A family of hydrocarbons. Terpenes are basically oils and oily resins produced from plants, their major source in the atmosphere. They are released by pine trees and create the blue haze observable over forests. Some terpenes are also produced in automobile exhausts. Terpenes can be refined to manufacture turpentine and other solvents. Like other hydrocarbons, terpenes can produce lung irritation or may promote cancers after long-term exposure.

THALLIUM (Tl). A soft, bluish-white toxic metal used in pesticides and insecticides. In the autumn of 1988, 127 children in the Ukrainian town of Chernovtsy (near the Soviet-Rumanian border) became ill and lost their hair. This sickness was traced to high doses of thallium in the air. Minute particles of the metal were probably carried into the area by rains in July. To stem the thallium poisoning, several metal refining operations in the surrounding areas of the Ukraine were closed down.

Exposure to thallium particles in the air can cause hair loss, joint and muscle pains, central nervous system effects, and kidney failure.

THERMAL POLLUTION. The addition of excess heat to the atmosphere as a result of human activities. The heat energy released by human activities from urban and industrial sources affects the earth's overall heat patterns. Surface temperatures in cities usually exceed those in rural areas. Power plants and industrial plants both release heat and moisture. This causes clouds to form that trap heat in the lower atmosphere.

A study published in November 1988 concluded that the earth's climate had warmed 1 degree Fahrenheit over levels recorded in 1900. Many scientists believe that the higher readings are indicative of worldwide warming trends. See also **GLOBAL WARMING**.

THREE–MILE ISLAND DISASTER. See **DISASTERS, POL-LUTION–RELATED.**

TIN (Sn). A gray crystalline metallic element. Tin is an air pollutant because tin dust from ore refining and industrial processes finds its way into the atmosphere. In its pure state tin is not considered toxic, but some compounds release toxic fumes into the atmosphere. Many tin compounds produce lung irritation and skin rashes.

TOBACCO SMOKE. Smoke from cigarettes, cigars, and pipes.

Tobacco smoke is one of the most controversial air pollutants. It contains more than 200 different chemical substances. These include unburned carbon, hydrocarbon gases and tars, carbon monoxide, nitrogen oxides, and many other particles and gases known to be carcinogenic. Nicotine is the principal drug in tobacco smoke.

Smoking causes more premature deaths than any other health behavior. The Centers for Disease Control studies show that a smoker's life is cut short by about twenty years. Smoking causes more deaths than alcohol and drug abuse combined.

The children of mothers who smoke also suffer many health problems. Low birth weight among newborns results from shorter gestation periods in pregnant women who smoke. Among newborn and older children, those exposed to tobacco smoke show an increased mortality rate from respiratory and other diseases.

Smoking has also been found to be a leading cause of heart disease, emphysema, and other deadly diseases. Passive, or sidestream, smoke has also emerged as a health hazard to nonsmokers who inhale secondhand smoke from others.

TOLUENE ($C_6H_5CH_3$; also called **METHYLBENZENE**). A colorless, liquid hydrocarbon, it is a common air contaminant. Commercial preparations of toluene usually have small amounts of benzene as an impurity. It is used as a solvent in many compounds. These include explosives (TNT, for example), solvents used in office typing correction fluids, and dyes. Toluene has been linked to anemia and to impaired bone marrow function. Victims of acute poisoning have recovered after exposure has terminated.

TOXIC CHEMICALS. Chemicals that are poisonous to plants, animals, and humans. They come from many organic and inorganic chemical sources and include many compounds of the classes of aldehydes, sulfates, nitrates, and oxides. Industrial solvents used in cleaning processes may emit dangerous hydrocarbon fumes such as benzene, toluene, and xylene.

Many toxic substances are produced in automobile exhausts and from other forms of combustion, including tobacco smoke. Industrial operations introduce a host of toxic metals, solvents, and other chemicals used or produced in various processes. The use of herbicides, insecticides, and pesticides is another source of aerosols and toxic chemicals. Spraying with these chemicals leaves poisonous residues and creates aerosols of the substances. Even building and decorating materials may outgas toxic vapors of formaldehyde, for example.

Various pollutants can produce degrees of discomfort or disease, but toxic chemicals in the environment can accumulate in the body and produce organ, nerve, and tissue damage, serious illnesses, and even death.

Sometimes low-level exposure to toxic chemicals in humans affects the brain and nervous system. The exposure may influence reaction times, speed of comprehension, and manual dexterity. (5, 26, 27, 35, 37)

TRICHLOROETHANE (CH_3CCl_3; also called **1,1,1–TRI-CHLOROETHANE** and **METHYLCHLOROFORM**). A colorless, volatile liquid. Trichloroethane cuts through grease and is used in various industrial cleaning processes. Often it is a substitute for carbon tetrachloride.

In low concentrations, exposure may lead to loss of coordination and balance or to mild irritation of eyes and nasal passages. Headaches and liver and kidney damage are other health hazards. Unconsciousness and death may result from continued high level exposure.

TRICHLOROTRIFLUOROETHANE (FCl_2CClF_2). A volatile, clear, colorless liquid. It is a CFC used as a refrigerant and is nonflammable. Freon is a trade name given to commercial preparations of the substance. Trichlorotrifluoroethane is a good solvent for grease and oil. It does not damage most materials with which it comes into contact. At 204° C (400° F) it decomposes to chlorine and fluorine. These gases are highly corrosive and can also destroy ozone molecules in the ozone layer. Trichlorotrifluoroethane has a low level of toxicity. In confined places, however, it can asphyxiate since it displaces the oxygen available for respiration.

TROPOSPHERE. See **ATMOSPHERE.**

U

ULTRAVIOLET RADIATION. Radiation from the sun with wavelengths shorter than those of visible light and longer than those of X rays. Much of the ultraviolet radiation that comes from the sun is absorbed in the ozone layer before it ever reaches the earth's surface. Some ozone is formed when oxygen molecules (O_2) absorb ultraviolet radiation and accept an additional oxygen atom to form ozone (O_3). This is known as photochemical oxidation and is one of the ways smog is formed.

A certain amount of ultraviolet radiation is necessary for health. Vitamin D plays a part in the body's use of the radiation. But overexposure to ultraviolet rays is dangerous. Over 80 percent of skin cancers are due to exposure to ultraviolet light. In the future the number of cases of cancer may increase. This will be the result of higher levels of ultraviolet radiation reaching the earth because of the thinning of the atmospheric ozone shield. See also **OZONE LAYER, PHOTOCHEMICAL AIR POLLUTION,** and **SMOG.**

URBAN AIR POLLUTION. Air contamination found in cities. City air almost always has a heavier load of contaminants than rural air. The principal sources of pollution in most cities are exhaust gases from gasoline and diesel engines. Automobile exhaust produces carbon monoxide, hydrocarbons, uncombusted fuel components, lead particles, soot, and products of incomplete oxidation such as the family of aldehydes, benzo(a)pyrene, and nitrogen oxides. Industries located in and around cities add tons of air pollutants of all kinds.

The urban environment itself, with its massive buildings, paved streets, and heating systems, affects the way radiation is received from the sun. In cities 5 to 30 percent less radiation is received from the sun, and 5 to 10 percent more clouds are formed. Cities experience 100 percent more fog in winter, 30 percent more fog in summer, and 5 to 10 percent more precipitation all year around than nearby rural areas.

V

VENTILATION SYSTEMS. Systems designed to circulate air and to bring fresh air into buildings. Ironically, the systems often cause some indoor pollution. Those that circulate stale air may increase and spread any air pollutants that are present. Improperly located air intakes may draw additional pollutants such as automobile exhaust from outside. A faulty ventilation system is often the cause of "sick-building syndrome."

The dust that builds up in ventilator filters can be an ideal place for disease-carrying organisms to grow. The organic pollutants found there may include particles of animal and insect excreta, pollen grains, molds, fungi, bacteria, and viruses. Many of these biological pollutants can cause allergic reactions or infections in some people. Legionnaire's Disease is thought to have been first caused by bacteria growing in a hotel's ventilation system.

An efficient ventilation system, properly maintained, cleaned, and disinfected periodically, should change the air in a building several times an hour and should contribute to the health and comfort of building users. See also **LEGIONNAIRE'S DISEASE** and **SICK–BUILDING SYNDROME.** (15)

VINYL CHLORIDE (CH_2CHCl; abbreviated **CVC**; also known as **CHLOROETHYLENE** or **CHLOROETHANE**). A colorless, flammable liquid or gas. It is used in industry to produce floor tiles, plastic containers and wraps, electrical insulation, phonograph records, and other forms of polyvinyl chloride (PVC).

On direct contact, the substance causes burns by rapid evaporation and the freezing of tissue. There is also evidence of damage to bone and to the circulatory system. Vinyl chloride is carcinogenic and has been found to cause liver cancer.

VIRAL POLLUTION. Airborne contamination containing viruses. Viruses are simple primitive organisms. They consist of little more than a protein sheath wrapped around a piece of genetic material that is capable of reproducing itself. Viruses are amoung the smallest and lightest particles that are present in the air. They measure from 0.01 to 0.1 micron in size. Viruses cannot move by themselves, but they can "hitch" rides on dust, pollen, grains, spores, and other organic matter. Sometimes insects may carry contagious viral diseases.

Viruses can infect humans, animals, and plants and may be spread to other organisms through the air. Viruses cause disease when they enter the system of plants and animals. They replicate, trigger infections, and sometimes cause death. The virus that causes AIDS is not an airborne virus. See also **INDOOR AIR POLLUTION** and **VENTILATION SYSTEMS.** (15)

VISIBILITY. The clearness or transparency of the air. Visibility is affected by the levels of pollution in the atmosphere. Particulate matter, nitrogen dioxide, and sulfur oxide decrease visibility. Particles in the air also serve as condensation nuclei for the formation of fog, clouds, and smog that block light and visibility. These conditions present a hazard to operators of aircraft, automobiles, and boats.

A sun photometer is an instrument that determines how much the sun's rays are obscured by atmospheric pollutants. The photometer's precise measurements give an accurate indication of the degree of pollution in the air.

VOLCANIC ACTIVITY. All volcanoes produce gases in their magma. Volcanoes contribute to atmospheric levels of water vapor, carbon dioxide, and dust. Carbon dioxide and hydrogen sulfide are usually released harmlessly through fissures and faults in the rocks or in hot springs or geysers. But sometimes the gases can build up to form gas pockets that may explode if they become agitated.

Active volcanoes produce dust that is carried by the wind. This dust is known as volcanic ash. Sometimes volcanoes erupt with such force that dust and ash are sent high into the stratosphere. Asamayama, a large Japanese volcano, erupted in 1783, affecting clouds the world over. When the island volcano Krakatoa erupted in 1883, some volcanic dust samples were collected in Holland, halfway around the world.

Dust from the eruption of Mount St. Helens in 1980 spread over vast portions of the northern hemisphere. For weeks fine white dust from Mount St. Helens settled all over North America—even on the east coast of the United States.

Volcanic eruptions cause the heaviest damage to the layer of the atmosphere known as the stratosphere. Ash-laden clouds containing particles of rock and high concentrations of sulfur dioxide can create an umbrella of particles. This dust cover cuts off sunshine and reduces ground temperatures over an entire hemisphere for periods of months. The year 1816 was known as the year without a summer. Dust from a volcanic explosion in the Pacific Ocean cut off so much light that snow and ice formed in New England in July.

Now scientists believe that volcanic eruptions are partially responsible for damage to the ozone layer. Volcanoes annually release eleven million tons of hydrogen chloride and six million tons of hydrogen fluoride. Both of these gases destroy atmospheric ozone. See also **OZONE LAYER.**

W

WATER VAPOR. A clear, odorless, colorless gas. Water vapor is water in its gaseous state. Water vapor is one of the most important components of air and also the most variable. The substance is present in fogs, smogs, mists, and clouds. Water vapor cleans dust and pollutants from the air when it becomes precipitation. Water vapor influences weather and all meteorological processes.

The size and number of condensed water vapor particles in the air affect visibility. Water vapor is also responsible for the formation of acid rain. Particles of pollutants act as condensation nuclei where vapor condenses and water droplets form. The nature of the condensation nuclei determines the acidity of the rain. See also **ACID PRECIPITATION** and **CONDENSATION NUCLEI.**

WORKPLACE, POLLUTION IN THE. Factories and industrial settings are likely places where air pollution occurs. But more and more air pollution is occurring in the unlikely surroundings of the business office. Poorly designed and maintained ventilation systems add to the problem.

Spokespeople from OSHA said in January 1989 that they could save 700 lives a year in the workplace. The lives could be saved by limiting worker exposure to 164 substances newly identified as hazardous and by tightening the limits on 212 substances already recognized as hazardous. The new substances include grain dust, gasoline fumes, butane, acrylic acid, and ethylene glycol (a component of antifreeze). Dangerous substances previously recognized include chloroform, carbon monoxide, hydrogen cyanide, and perchloroethylene. Methyl chloride recently topped the list of the most prevalent contaminants released into the air by industry. Critics of the new guidelines state that other workplace hazards have not yet been recognized. They cite pollutants such as cadmium and tobacco smoke as dangerous substances that should be added to OSHA's list. See also **INDOOR AIR POLLUTION** and **SICK–BUILDING SYNDROME.**

X

XYLENE (C_8H_{10}; also known as **DIMETHYLBENZENE**). A colorless, oily hydrocarbon liquid. The presence of xylene in the atmosphere is largely due to automobile exhaust. Xylene is in the air in low concentrations and is only mildly toxic. It is an irritant by contact or inhalation.

Z

ZINC (Zn). A bluish-white crystalline metal. The manufacture of metal containers and brass releases zinc particles into the atmosphere. Zinc is also released in fly ash. Particles of zinc compounds enter the atmosphere naturally as rock or other materials containing zinc weather.

Zinc solids are only slightly toxic, but heating zinc releases fumes that can cause aching, flulike symptoms. In high concentration, zinc chloride fumes have caused lung damage. Zinc oxide dust can block the ducts of the glands that produce oils in the skin.

FOR FURTHER INFORMATION

GOVERNMENT AGENCIES

Bureau of Oceans and International Environmental and Scientific Affairs
Department of State
2201 C Street
Washington, DC 20520
(202) 634-3600

Centers for Disease Control
1600 Clifton Road NE
Atlanta, GA 30329
(404) 639-3311

The Council on Environmental Quality
722 Jackson Place NW
Washington, DC 20503
(202) 395-5750

Environmental Protection Agency (EPA)
Public Information Center
401 M Street SW
Washington, DC 20460
(202) 382-2090

The National Environmental Satellite Data and Information Service
1825 Connecticut Avenue
Washington, DC 20235
(202) 673-5594

National Oceanic and Atmospheric Administration (NOAA)
Office of Oceanic and Atmospheric Research
Department of Commerce
14th Street and Constitution Avenue NW
Washington, DC 20230
(202) 673-5594

Occupational Safety and Health Administration (OSHA)
Department of Labor
200 Constitution Avenue NW
Washington, DC 20210
(202) 523-6666

Occupational Safety and Health
Review Commission
1825 K Street NW
Washington, DC 20006
(202) 634-7960

Office of Science and Technology
Policy
Old Executive Office Building
Washington, DC 20506
(202) 377-2000

CONSUMER ORGANIZATIONS

**Environmental Action
Foundation**
1525 New Hampshire
  Avenue NW
Washington, DC 20036
(202) 745-4871

Environmental Defense Fund
1616 P Street NW
Suite 150
Washington, DC 20036
(202) 387-3500

Greenpeace Action
96 Spring Street
Third Floor
New York, NY 10012
(212) 941-0994

**Natural Resources Defense
Council**
1350 New York Avenue NW
Suite 300
Washington, DC 20005
(202) 783-7800

**Public Citizen Health Research
Group**
2000 P Street NW
Suite 700
Washington, DC 20036
(202) 293-9142

Worldwatch Institute
1776 Massachusetts Avenue NW
Washington, DC 20036
(202) 452-1999

REFERENCES

BOOKS

1. Allen, Oliver E. *Atmosphere.* Alexandria, VA, Time-Life Books, 1983.

2. Anthes, Richard, et al. *The Atmosphere.* Columbus, OH, Merrill Publishing Co., 1975.

3. Bernard, Harold W., Jr. *The Greenhouse Effect.* Cambridge, MA, Ballinger Publishing Co., 1980.

4. Breuer, George. *Air in Danger, Ecological Perspectives of the Atom.* (translated by Peter Fabian). Cambridge, England, Cambridge University Press, 1980.

5. Brown, Michael H. *The Toxic Cloud.* New York, Harper & Row, 1987.

6. Bryson, Reid A., and Thomas J. Murray. *Climates of Hunger: Mankind and the World's Changing Weather.* Madison, WI, University of Wisconsin Press, 1977.

7. Cannon, James S. *A Clear View: A Guide to Industrial Pollution Control.* New York, INFORM, 1975.

8. Carr, Donald E. *The Sky Is Still Falling.* New York, W.W. Norton, 1982.

9. Crone, Hugh. *Chemicals and Society: A Guide to the New Chemical Age.* Cambridge, England, Cambridge University Press, 1987.

10. Dadd, Debra L. *The Nontoxic Home: Protecting Yourself and Your Family from Everyday Toxics and Health Hazards.* Los Angeles, J.P. Tarcher, 1986.

11. Gallant, Roy A. *Earth's Changing Climate.* New York, Four Winds Press, 1979.

12. Gay, Kathlyn. *Acid Rain.* New York, Franklin Watts, 1983.

13. ———. *Silent Killers: Radon and Other Hazards.* New York, Franklin Watts, 1988.

14. Gough, Michael. *Dioxin, Agent Orange: The Facts.* New York, Plenum Press, 1986.

15. Greenfield, Ellen. *House Dangerous: Indoor Pollution in Your Home and Office and What You Can Do About It!* New York, Vintage Books, 1987.

16. Gribbin, John R. *Future Weather and the Greenhouse Effect.* New York, Delacorte Press/Eleanor Friede, 1982.

17. Kellogg, William W., and Robert Schware. *Climate Change and Society: Consequences of Increasing Carbon Dioxide.* Boulder, CO, Westview Press, 1981.

18. LaFavore, Michael. *Radon: The Invisible Threat.* Emmaus, PA, Rodale Press, Inc., 1987.

19. Leithe, Wolfgang. *The Analysis of Air Pollutants.* Ann Arbor, MI, Ann Arbor Science Publishers, 1970.

20. Meyer, Beat. *Indoor Air Quality.* Addison-Wesley Publishing Co., 1983.

21. Nations, James D. *Tropical Rainforests: Endangered Atmosphere.* New York, Franklin Watts, 1988.

22. Painter, Dean E. *Air Pollution Technology.* Englewood Cliffs, NJ, Reston Publishing Co., 1974.

23. Pringle, Laurence P. *Rain of Troubles: The Science and Politics of Acid Rain.* New York, Macmillan, 1988.

24. Riehl, Herbert. *Introduction to the Atmosphere.* New York, McGraw-Hill, 1978.

25. Ross, Richard D. *Air Pollution and Industry.* New York, Van Nostrand Reinhold, 1972.

26. Sax, N. Irving. *Industrial Pollution.* New York, Van Nostrand Reinhold, 1974.

27. Schieler, Leroy and Denis Pauzé. *Hazardous Materials.* New York, Van Nostrand Reinhold, 1976.

28. Schneider, Stephen H. *The Genesis Strategy: Climate and Global Survival.* New York, Plenum Press, 1976.

29. Seinfeld, John H. *Air Pollution: Physical and Chemical Fundamentals.* New York, McGraw-Hill, 1974.

30. Shriner, David S. et al., editors. *Atmospheric Sulfur Deposition: Environmental Impact and Health Effects.* Ann Arbor, MI, Ann Arbor Science Publishers, 1980.

31. Skinner, Brian J., editor. *Climates Past and Present.* Los Altos, CA, William Kaufmann, 1981.

32. Turiel, Isaac. *Indoor Air Quality and Human Health.* Stanford, CA, Stanford University Press, 1985.

33. Vesilind, P. Aarme and Jeffrey S. Pierce. *Environmental Pollution and Control* (2nd edition). Stoneham, MA, Butterworth, 1983.

34. Wark, Kenneth and Cecil F. Warner. *Air Pollution: Its Origins and Control.* New York, Harper and Row, 1976.

35. Weiss, Malcolm E. *Toxic Waste: Clean-up or Cover-up?* New York, Franklin Watts, 1984.

36. Williamson, Samuel J. *Fundamentals of Air Pollution.* Reading, MA, Addison-Wesley Publishing Co., 1973.

37. Zipko, Stephen J. *Toxic Threat: How Hazardous Substances Poison Our Lives.* New York, Messner, 1986.

NEWSPAPERS AND PERIODICALS

The newspapers and periodicals listed here regularly give significant coverage to the latest developments regarding the problem of air pollution: *Insight on the news; National Geographic; Natural History; Nature; The New York Times; Newsweek; Scientific American; Smithsonian; Time; U.S. News and World Report; U.S.A. Today; The Wall Street Journal.*

ABOUT THE AUTHOR

Cass R. Sandak is the author of nearly forty nonfiction books for children. He has written about the sciences, sports, holidays, engineering, exploration, and civilization. He has also written numerous articles on a variety of topics. The British Trust for Children's Literature named his book *The Arctic and Antarctic* one of 1988's Ten Best Books for Children.

The author is a summa cum laude graduate of Union College in Schenectady, New York, and did graduate work at the University of Pennsylvania. For several years, he has been a consultant in technical, scientific, and promotional writing for corporate clients. He is a member of Phi Beta Kappa and the Academy of American Poets.

Mr. Sandak divides his time between Manhattan and homes in upstate New York. In his free moments he enjoys traveling and is active in community affairs.